Advanced Introduction to International Intellectual Property

Elgar Advanced Introductions are stimulating and thoughtful introductions to major fields in the social sciences and law, expertly written by the world's leading scholars. Designed to be accessible yet rigorous, they offer concise and lucid surveys of the substantive and policy issues associated with discrete subject areas.

The aims of the series are two-fold: to pinpoint essential principles of a particular field, and to offer insights that stimulate critical thinking. By distilling the vast and often technical corpus of information on the subject into a concise and meaningful form, the books serve as accessible introductions for undergraduate and graduate students coming to the subject for the first time. Importantly, they also develop well-informed, nuanced critiques of the field that will challenge and extend the understanding of advanced students, scholars and policy-makers.

Titles in the series include:

Advanced Introduction to

International Intellectual Property

SUSY FRANKEL

Faculty of Law, Victoria University of Wellington, New Zealand

DANIEL J. GERVAIS

Vanderbilt University Law School, USA

Elgar Advanced Introductions

Cheltenham, UK • Northampton, MA, USA

Published by
Edward Elgar Publishing Limited
The Lypiatts
15 Lansdown Road
Cheltenham
Glos GL50 2JA
UK

Edward Elgar Publishing, Inc.
William Pratt House
9 Dewey Court
Northampton
Massachusetts 01060
USA

A catalogue record for this book
is available from the British Library

Library of Congress Control Number: 2015950290

ISBN 978 1 78347 049 5 (cased)
ISBN 978 1 78347 342 7 (paperback)
ISBN 978 1 78347 050 1 (eBook)

Typeset by Servis Filmsetting Ltd, Stockport, Cheshire

Printed and bound in Great Britain by
TJ International Ltd, Padstow, Cornwall

Contents

Introduction

This book is designed for students, researchers and practitioners of intellectual property (IP) interested in gaining an understanding of the international rules and the context in which domestic intellectual property policy issues must be understood. Law students and practitioners in almost any field will encounter intellectual property issues, and more often than not international rules are relevant for at least two reasons. First, they may explain the origin of a rule in domestic law, that is, meant to implement an international obligation. Second, but relatedly, international rules and their drafting history can be used to understand and interpret domestic rules. Policy makers implementing changes to their domestic intellectual property regime, often consider whether those changes are compatible with their international intellectual property obligations and draft their rules accordingly. Finally, in some countries international treaty rules will have direct application in domestic law. Hence, few businesses whether they are small or large, can operate without knowing how rules may differ in other territories to which they wish to export and with which they wish to enter into outsourcing or partnership agreements.

A structural and fundamental element of most international intellectual property instruments is the principle of national treatment, the essence of which is that courts, intellectual property offices and administrative agencies must treat foreigners no less favourably than their own nationals. To demonstrate national treatment's prevalence, the concept is provided for in three of the most important substantive instruments, namely the Paris Convention for the Protection of Industrial Property (Article 3(a)),[1] the Berne Convention for the Protection of Literary and Artistic Works

---

1 WIPO, Paris Convention for the Protection of Industrial Property, 20 March 1883, 828 U.N.T.S. 305, as last revised at the Stockholm Revision Conference 14 July 1967, www.wipo.int/treaties/en/text.jsp?file_id=287556; accessed 23 March 2015 (hereinafter Paris Convention).

(Article 5),[2] and the Agreement on Trade-Related Aspects of Intellectual Property Rights, better known as the TRIPS Agreement (Article 3).[3] We devote a section to national treatment later on.

Researchers of intellectual property in several areas frequently consider comparative differences in how IP issues are framed and solutions proposed or adopted in various countries and regions. This research often points to how the international system itself might be improved. It can also point to how national approaches to intellectual property law are often deeply embedded and framed within a national legal system and consequently such traditions are difficult to change (and it may even be undesirable to do so).

This book provides an advanced introduction to the international regime of intellectual property, which includes interpretation of international rules at the national level and examples of national laws that illustrate ways in which the international regime can be implemented. This book is written for those readers who already have some knowledge of intellectual property rules and concepts at the national and regional level, though it may also be suitable for those without such knowledge.

Our aim is to provide a thorough overview in a short book. For those wanting more detail on a particular subject, this book can be used in tandem with other books which are more detailed on specific subjects. Books dealing with only one of the many topics we cover, such as the history of the World Intellectual Property Organization (WIPO) or one of the many multilateral treaties, agreements and conventions, are often hundreds of pages long. This book provides an overview of the fundamentals of international intellectual property and the most important points in its current evolution. Where we felt it was appropriate without overwhelming the text or footnotes, we also point to sources containing more detailed information.

---

2 WIPO, Berne Convention for the Protection of Literary and Artistic Works, 9 September 1886, 828 U.N.T.S. 221, as last revised 24 July 1971, www.wipo.int/treaties/en/text.jsp?file_id=283698, accessed 23 March 2015 (hereinafter Berne Convention).

3 WTO, Agreement Establishing the World Trade Organization, Annex 1C: Agreement on Trade-Related Aspects of Intellectual Property Rights, 15 April 1994, 1869 U.N.T.S. 299, at www.wto.org/english/docs_e/legal_e/27-trips_01_e.htm, accessed 23 March 2015 (hereinafter TRIPS Agreement). As will become apparent below, this Agreement is more significant because of its scope and its enforceability.

This Advanced Introduction examines the principal intellectual property instruments, their history and context, as well as the main institutions that administer them.[4]

The functions of international intellectual property agreements vary from agreement to agreement; however, each one seeks to promote norms that can be grouped into three categories:

(1) Setting minimum standards of protection that must be adhered to in each member state. We refer to those as substantive instruments.
(2) Setting up a framework to enable the creation of an intellectual property right in one member state to result in, or assist in, creation of an intellectual property right in another member state – in other words, harmonizing the descriptions of goods and services for purposes of registration. We refer to those as classification instruments.
(3) Easing the process by which a right holder may apply to register his or her intellectual property right (where registration is required) by creating multilateral registration mechanisms and authorities. We refer to those as procedural instruments.

Before moving on, we should clarify a small but important terminological matter. Countries party to the Berne and Paris Conventions are members of the Berne and Paris Unions, respectively. Those Unions have their own procedural rules, and each one has its own Assembly. By contrast, no country can ratify or adhere to the TRIPS Agreement.[5] Any *member* of the World Trade Organization (WTO) is bound by TRIPS as Annex 1C of the Agreement Establishing the World Trade Organization.[6] No reservations are permitted. Not all WTO members are countries. Some are trade territories (such as Macao); others are intergovernmental organizations (such as the European Union).

---

4 We use the term "instrument" in this book in a generic sense that encompasses international treaties and conventions, international and regional agreements and intellectual property chapters or parts of broader international treaties and arrangements.

5 Ratification follows the signature of an international instrument; adhesion happens when a country that has not signed an instrument accepts to be bound by it. Signature without ratification is not devoid of legal effect in public international law but that discussion is beyond the scope of this book.

6 The WTO Agreement and its various annexes were part of the Uruguay Round package, which ended the Uruguay Round of Multilateral Trade Negotiations. See Section [2.2.1].

This book is divided into five chapters. We first describe the role of the two major multilateral institutions of intellectual property (Chapter 1). Chapter 2 outlines the major instruments of international intellectual property. In Chapter 3 we explain some key and fundamental concepts and features of international intellectual property. In Chapter 4 we provide a sector by sector (copyright, patents, trademarks, etc.) analysis of current norms. Finally, in Chapter 5 we provide analysis of a number of evolving issues in international intellectual property, which can also be used, in a teaching context, as discussion and review topics.

1 The institutions and actors of international intellectual property

The two main multilateral intergovernmental institutions in the field of intellectual property at the multilateral level are WIPO and the WTO. A number of other intergovernmental institutions are also active in the field, including the United Nations Educational, Scientific and Cultural Organization (UNESCO) on matters such as cultural heritage and education; the World Health Organization (WHO) on matters concerning pharmaceutical and medical research and access to medicines; the International Labour Office (ILO) on matters concerning the rights of performing artists; and the secretariat of the Convention on Biological Diversity (CBD) and its Nagoya Protocol on matters relating to uses of biological and genetic resources and the protection of related traditional knowledge.

A number of non-governmental organizations (NGOs) are also extremely active at the international level.[7] They include organizations representing "right holders" such as pharmaceutical companies, entertainment conglomerates, and luxury brand owners, but also small inventors, songwriters, film makers, actors and performing artists. Some represent indigenous communities that have an interest in protecting their indigenous cultural and medicinal heritage. Even within an industry, not everyone may have similar interests. For example, the software industry includes companies seeking high levels of protection of intellectual property, while others have business models that rely on "open source" software or the possibility of using material created by others. Within the pharmaceutical industry, the companies that spend some part of their profits on research and drug development

---

7 A list of international NGOs accredited at WIPO is at WIPO, "Accredited Observers, International Non-Governmental Organizations", www.wipo.int/members/en/organizations.jsp?type=NGO_ INT, accessed 22 April 2015. As of March 2015, there were 252 such organizations (in addition, 74 national NGOs are also WIPO-accredited). Many of these are authors' or intellectual property owner organizations. Unlike WIPO, the WTO has been reluctant to admit NGOs to participate in its meetings.

do not always see "eye-to-eye" with those that produce generic drugs (drugs that are not or no longer protected by a patent). Other NGOs represent users of intellectual property mostly or entirely generated by others. They may be consumer groups, Internet-based enterprises, such as search engines or cloud services, and organizations defending access to culture, science and medicines.

1.1 The World Intellectual Property Organization (WIPO)

To address the concern that different countries did not provide similar (and in some cases any effective) levels of intellectual property protection (in particular of foreign intellectual property) and consequently that inventions, copyright works and other forms of intellectual property could be replicated in other countries without payment or attribution, the organization that would become WIPO was established in the late nineteenth century.[8] Known as the United International Bureau for the Protection of Intellectual Property (or, under the French acronym, BIRPI),[9] it would serve as the administrative structure on which WIPO was founded in 1968. BIRPI "united" the International Bureau established by the Paris Convention in 1883 and the Bureau established by the Berne Convention three years later. BIRPI, unlike WIPO, was not part of the United Nations. In fact, it was operating under the supervision of the Swiss government.

Why was BIRPI created in the 1880s? At the time, international trade was still in its infancy and limited mostly to raw and primary goods and materials. Increasingly, however, it was starting to involve machinery, books and various trademarked goods. Many creators and owners of intellectual property felt that greater international exposure meant a greater likelihood that people in other countries would

---

8 See WIPO, *WIPO – A Brief History*, at www.wipo.int/about-wipo/en/history.html, accessed 23 March 2015.

9 WIPO describes its predecessor, the United International Bureau for the Protection of Intellectual Property (best known by its French acronym BIRPI) usefully on its website, www.wipo.int/treaties/en/general/, accessed 5 October 2015, as thus: "Based in Berne, Switzerland, with a staff of seven, this small organization was the predecessor of the World Intellectual Property Organization of today – a dynamic entity with 188 member States, a staff that now numbers some 938, from 95 countries around the world, and with a mission and a mandate that are constantly growing." The BIRPI acronym above (the predecessor organization of WIPO) includes the word "united" because it administered both industrial property and authors' rights.

use their intellectual property without their consent.[10] The need for international protection of intellectual property became evident in particular when foreign exhibitors refused to attend the International Exhibition of Inventions in Vienna in 1873 because they feared their ideas and inventions would be stolen and commercially exploited elsewhere.

It would be accurate – if perhaps overly simplistic – to say that the Paris Convention's birth in 1883 can be attributed to these large international fairs to which countries brought their most advanced machines and inventions, including the famous Paris Fair of 1900, which had previously led to the construction of the Eiffel Tower. In fact, as we will see below, the Paris Convention still contains a number of provisions that seem much more relevant in a world of international trade in physical goods, including goods travelling by sea. The Paris Convention deals with what was then referred to as *industrial property*, namely trademarks, patents, industrial designs and confidential information.

At around the same time, a philosophical movement born in the wake of the Enlightenment led (in countries such as France and Germany) to the recognition of a special role for authors of "works of the mind". What we might today call the creative class rose to prominence. The special nature of their contribution and the special place of books, music, painting (and later film etc.) led to adoption of laws protecting authors' rights. In 1886, after a major campaign led by a well-known French author Victor Hugo – whose works still find audiences (*Les Misérables* comes to mind) – a second major international convention emerged in the capital of Switzerland, Berne. It was what we now call the Berne Convention.

BIRPI organized a number of revision conferences to update the two main instruments it administered, namely the Paris and Berne Conventions, as well as a number of procedural and classification instruments. At the last such conference, held in Stockholm (Sweden) in 1967, the Agreement Establishing WIPO was signed. That Agreement went into effect in 1970 and the new organization, WIPO, took over from BIRPI. Still today, the WIPO secretariat is referred

---

10 The drafting history of the TRIPS Agreement (see Section [2.2.1]) shows that the Agreement was reached because of the concerns, primarily of developed countries, that trade increased the likelihood of counterfeiting of intellectual property products.

to in a number of official documents as the "International Bureau", reflecting its BIRPI heritage. WIPO, as the organization administering the Berne and Paris Conventions, organizes the meetings of the Berne and Paris Union Assemblies, as well as its own General Assembly, usually all held together in September of each year as the WIPO Governing Bodies meetings. In 1974, WIPO became one of 16 specialized agencies of the United Nations.[11]

In the late 1970s and all during the 1980s, 1990s and 2000s, WIPO was active on several fronts. A significant increase in membership arose through countries becoming members of WIPO (by adhering to the Convention establishing WIPO) and often of the Paris and/or Berne Conventions as well. As of November 2015, WIPO had 188 member countries, while 168 and 176 countries had adhered to the Berne and Paris Conventions, respectively. This great increase in membership led to a major increase in technical assistance to developing and other countries wishing to develop their intellectual property laws and administration. WIPO was also active on other fronts, helping to negotiate major treaties to facilitate international applications for trademarks, patents and other rights, including the 1970 Patent Cooperation Treaty and the Madrid system, renewed in 1989 and allowing trademark applicants to protect their rights through registration in several countries and territories. We discuss these in greater detail later on.

Since 1994 WIPO has adjusted to an environment where the trade aspects of intellectual property have been negotiated under the auspices of another international organization. In April 1994, after seven years of official negotiations, the Agreement Establishing the WTO was concluded in Marrakesh, Morocco. The TRIPS Agreement was Annex 1C of the WTO Agreement. The TRIPS Agreement incorporates most of the substantive norms of the Paris and Berne Conventions, adds or modifies some of those norms and subjects the package (that is, pre-existing Paris and Berne Convention norms and new TRIPS norms) to the WTO Dispute Settlement System.

Since 1994, there has been relatively little effective norm development work in the field of intellectual property at the WTO. An amendment

---

11 Agreement between WIPO and the United Nations, signed on 21 January 1975, entered into force on 17 December 1974. Other specialized agencies at the time included the above-mentioned ILO and WHO, but also, for example, the Food and Agriculture Organization (FAO) and the International Telecommunications Union (ITU).

to the TRIPS Agreement was adopted in 2006 to permit export of pharmaceutical products to least developed countries under a compulsory licensing regime. Work on a possible register for geographical indications (GIs) was also undertaken, as were studies on possible changes to the patent system to reflect the origin or ownership of genetic material used in certain inventions. We return to these matters later on.

Since the formation of the WTO, by contrast, WIPO has hosted ongoing discussions about harmonization of patent and trademark law. It has finalized treaties in relation to digital copyright and performers' rights (1996), the protection of audio-visual performers (2012) and exceptions to copyright for the visually impaired (2013). WIPO has also established an ongoing programme of international negotiations on the protection of traditional knowledge, genetic resources and traditional cultural expressions, and a "development agenda" focusing mostly on how best to adapt the international intellectual property regime to the needs of developing nations.

WIPO has an agreement with the WTO to "mutually support" each other on intellectual property matters.[12] This support is evident in dispute settlement where the WTO formally consults WIPO regarding intellectual property norms.[13] It is also significant that parts of WIPO's treaties are incorporated into the intellectual property agreement that the WTO administers: the TRIPS Agreement[14] discussed below.

1.2   The World Trade Organization (WTO)

1.2.1   Establishment of the WTO

The Uruguay Round of Multilateral Trade Negotiations started in a convention centre overlooking the beaches of Punta del Este, Uruguay in 1986. The discussions were held under the auspices of the General Agreement on Tariffs and Trade (GATT), which is effectively the predecessor of the WTO.[15] As a result of the Uruguay Round, the

---

12 WTO–WIPO Co-operation Agreement, World Trade Organization, Geneva 22 December 1995; see "Approval of Agreements with Intergovernmental Organizations", World Intellectual Property Organization (WIPO); www.wipo.int/edocs/mdocs/govbody/en/wo_cc_48/wo_cc_48_2.doc, accessed 30 March 2015.

13 We discuss this further in Section [3.2] Principles of Treaty Interpretation.

14 TRIPS Agreement, Articles 2 and 9 (i).

15 General Agreement on Tariffs and Trade (1947) 55 U.N.T.S. 194 (hereinafter GATT). The GATT was a legal instrument, not an intergovernmental organization as such. It was, however,

WTO's mandate goes well beyond the GATT's previous focus on trade in goods. The WTO's reach now extends to services and intellectual property. The WTO describes itself as:

> The only global international organization dealing with the rules of trade between nations. At its heart are the WTO agreements, negotiated and signed by the bulk of the world's trading nations and ratified in their parliaments. The goal is to help producers of goods and services, exporters, and importers conduct their business.[16]

The WTO's overall objective is to lower barriers to international trade. In the case of goods it does this by converting non-tariff barriers to tariffs and then the members negotiate to lower tariffs. In relation to goods and services members of the WTO agree to give market access, on certain terms, to other members. Consequently, goods that embody intellectual property rights are more freely and widely circulated throughout the world, and cross-border licensing, outsourcing of intellectual property rights and foreign direct investment (FDI) in intellectual property-based products and services has increased. Together, these factors – and the global nature of the Internet – have created more opportunities for global trade and distribution of intellectual property. With that expansion there is greater potential infringement of foreign intellectual property rights and some have felt a greater need for protection. Consequently, the TRIPS Agreement also includes minimum standards relating to criminal and civil enforcement of intellectual property rights. With the greater need for protection has come a greater need for access opportunities to intellectual property works and related products and services. As we discuss later, increasing the level of protection of intellectual property has costs and has led to a greater need for appropriately crafted flexibilities.

The TRIPS Agreement contains a set of minimum legal standards that countries must implement in their national legislation. These minimum standards are coupled with voluntary exceptions and general principles about non-discrimination and the purposes and objectives of the Agreement. The structure of TRIPS contrasts with WTO

administered by a Geneva-based secretariat functioning more or less as a typical intergovernmental organization. As part of the formation of the WTO GATT 1947 was retained, General Agreement on Tariffs and Trade (GATT), 15 April 1994, Marrakesh Agreement Establishing the World Trade Organization, Annex 1A, 1867 U.N.T.S. 187, 33 ILM 1153 (1994).

16 WTO, *Understanding the WTO*, www.wto.org/english/thewto_e/whatis_e/tif_e/fact1_e.htm, accessed 30 March 2015.

agreements in other areas, which typically address the reduction of tariffs and other trade barriers rather than imposing minimum legal standards providing minimum rights to various persons (patent owners etc.). Another facet of mixing intellectual property and trade is that developed countries are the main producers of the intellectual property goods and services that TRIPS protects, while in the realm of trade in other goods, developing countries are also major exporters (oil, sugar, textiles, fruit, etc.). This imbalance has had political and social repercussions.

The drive of much of the developed world to expand intellectual property protection in the international trade framework has thus been met with criticism, particularly in the field of patent law, where the TRIPS Agreement has been regarded as responsible, for example, for having prevented nations from being able to afford certain pharmaceuticals. We explore this and other criticisms later in the book.

An important part of the WTO is the Council for TRIPS, which is the body that discusses and manages ongoing TRIPS issues within the WTO structure, subject to decisions by bodies higher in the WTO hierarchy (the General Council and Decisions made at Ministerial level).

1.2.2   The WTO dispute settlement process

The WTO administers its own dispute settlement system. The "code of civil procedure" the WTO uses is the Understanding on Rules and Procedures Governing the Settlement of Disputes, known as the Dispute Settlement Understanding (DSU), which was Annex 2 of the Agreement Establishing the WTO. The WTO Dispute Settlement Body (DSB), which includes representatives from all WTO members, administers the process. The DSB is made up of the individual members of the WTO.

When a WTO member advises the DSB of a possible dispute with another member, the dispute becomes a matter of public record. Consultations must take place and a surprisingly high number of disputes are settled at that stage. If consultations fail, the member who had notified the WTO of the dispute can ask that a panel (usually of three independent experts) be established. This typically happens in consultation with the WTO secretariat and the parties. WTO members not party to the dispute can ask to join as third parties. Once a panel has been established, it will receive briefs from parties and proceed to one or more hearings. NGOs and others may file briefs but there is no guarantee that they will be read or considered by the panel.

Decisions of this panel can be appealed to the Appellate Body. Panels are formed as disputes arise; whereas the Appellate Body is a permanent body. If a panel or the Appellate Body finds that a member's law is not compliant with the TRIPS Agreement, the DSB recommends that the member's laws be brought into compliance with TRIPS.

More specifically, the DSU establishes the process outlined in Figure 1.1.

The panel issues a report – not a "decision".[17] The report becomes binding once the DSB adopts it. That said, the DSU provides that panel and Appellate Body reports are adopted unless there is a consensus not to do so, a situation known as the negative consensus rule. Such a situation is unlikely because it requires the party that "won" the dispute to agree not to adopt the report. This default adoption rule means that reports are almost always adopted. All TRIPS related reports have been adopted. In many TRIPS Agreement disputes there is not necessarily one winner and one loser; rather each party wins and loses on some issues. Of course, this does not have to be the case, but it is prevalent in reports of disputes relating to the TRIPS Agreement and it perhaps reflects the role of the WTO as an international negotiating body not just a dispute settlement body.

Although time limits are placed on compliance with panel or Appellate Body findings, the main enforcement mechanism is trade retaliation (such as the imposition of tariffs) or the threat thereof. Compliance can take many forms. In the case of a dispute concerning United States' copyright law that allowed for uncompensated playing of music in certain restaurants and cafes, discussed below, the United States has not repealed the relevant part of its law as the DSB recommended and is unlikely ever to do so for internal political reasons. Rather, it pays the European Union compensation. Compensation is supposed to be a

---

17 In practice, a draft of the report is circulated to parties for comments before the official report is made public.

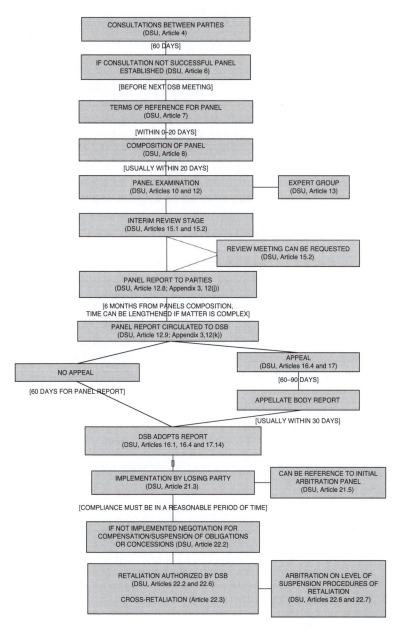

Figure 1.1   Overview of the World Trade Organization DSU process

short-term alternative in the WTO system, but in this case it was paid for several years.[18]

If a WTO member found to be in violation of its obligations fails to modify its legislation or practice, the other side may ask for the right to impose cross-retaliatory measures. Cross-retaliation means that a violation of the TRIPS Agreement may lead to the imposition of trade sanctions in areas other than intellectual property. Conversely, a violation of rules unrelated to intellectual property may lead to sanctions under TRIPS. The DSB has permitted the use of cross-retaliation in the context of the TRIPS Agreement (as a remedy for breaches of other WTO law).[19] Ecuador was permitted to suspend TRIPS Agreement obligations (called concessions in the WTO compliance context);[20] Antigua was permitted to suspend TRIPS Agreement concessions against the United States after winning a dispute in relation to the prevention of online gambling services;[21] and Brazil was permitted to suspend TRIPS concessions against the United States after winning a dispute about subsidies of cotton.[22] None of these suspensions of intellectual property obligations took place, but the threat of doing so seems to be at least for some a powerful systemic tool. For large countries, such as Brazil, the reality of possible suspension can be a powerful negotiation tool to extract some kind of remedy. In fact, after Brazil was granted the possibility of cross-retaliation because the United States

18 Understanding on Rules and Procedures Governing the Settlement of Disputes, 15 April 1994, Marrakesh Agreement Establishing the World Trade Organization, Annex 2, (1994) 1869 U.N.T.S. 401, HR Doc No. 103–315 at 1654 (hereinafter, DSU). Article 22(1) states "compensation . . . [is] a temporary measure".

19 In relation to other trade agreements, such as GATT, this is referred to as suspending concessions, rather than obligations.

20 WTO Appellate Body Report, *European Communities – Regime for the Importation, Sale and Distribution of Bananas*, WT/DS27/AB/R, (25 September 1997), (*EC Bananas*).

21 See WTO Appellate Body Report, *United States – Measures Affecting the Cross-border Supply of Gambling and Betting Services*, WT/DS285/AB/R, (7 April 2005); see also Decision by the Arbitrator, *Recourse to Arbitration by the United States under Article 22.6 of the DSU*, WT/DS285/ARB, (21 December 2007). In that dispute, however, Antigua did not suspend such concessions after post-DSB negotiations. There has been a range of intellectual property disputes brought before the DSB, some of which are discussed below in context with the type of intellectual property protection to which they relate.

22 Decision by the Arbitrator, *United States – Subsidies on Upland Cotton – Recourse to Arbitration by the United States under Article 22.6 of the DSU and Article 4.11 of the SCM Agreement*, WT/DS267/ARB/1, (31 August 2009); Decision by the Arbitrator, *United States – Subsidies on Upland Cotton – Recourse to Arbitration by the United States under Article 22.6 of the DSU and Article 7.10 of the SCM Agreement*, WT/DS267/ARB/2 and Corr.1, (31 August 2009), (*US – Cotton Subsidies*).

had not brought its law, relating to cotton subsidies, into line with the Appellate Body's recommendations, the threat of cross-retaliation seemed effective. Brazil and the United States reached an agreement. In contrast, the dispute between Antigua and the United States has been going on longer but the United States seems unresponsive to the comparatively lesser threat of Antiguan cross-retaliation.

Finally, it is worth noting that there is no principle of *stare decisis* (binding precedent) in WTO law.[23] That said, a kind of "WTO jurisprudence" is emerging. Understandably, dispute settlement panels strive to maintain consistency with previous reports and frequently refer in great detail to findings of prior panels.[24] Yet, as John Jackson has pointed out, there are "several specific instances in the GATT jurisprudence, where panels have consciously decided to depart from the results of a prior panel".[25] The Appellate Body has pointed out that a panel would have to have cogent reasons to differ from an Appellate Body decision.[26]

---

23 See, in general, I. Brownlie, *Principles of Public International Law*, Oxford: Clarendon Press 1998, at 19–22. Cf. J. H. Jackson, *The Jurisprudence of GATT and the WTO – Insights on Treaty Law and Economic Relations*, Cambridge: Cambridge University Press 2000, at 127.

24 Panel reports might refer to so-called "dispute settlement practice". See for instance WTO Panel Report, *United States – Section 110(5) of US Copyright Act*, WT/DS160/R, (15 May 2000), (*US – 110(5)*), at [6.13], [6.111], [6.162], [6.185], [6.231].

25 See J. H. Jackson, *The Jurisprudence of GATT and the WTO – Insights on Treaty Law and Economic Relations*, Cambridge: Cambridge University Press 2000, at 127.

26 WTO Appellate Body Report, *United States – Final Anti-Dumping Measures on Stainless Steel from Mexico*, WT/DS344/AB/R, (30 April 2008), at [160].

2 The major instruments of international intellectual property

Other than the TRIPS Agreement (administered by the WTO), there are 15 multilateral instruments administered by WIPO currently in force that WIPO considers as "intellectual property protection" instruments, as opposed to those it refers to as "global protection systems" instruments (basically those providing for international registration at WIPO) and those it categorizes as "classification" instruments (providing an information organizing function allowing applications to be indexed and more easily retrieved).

The texts of all those treaties are all available on the WIPO website. To see if a country is party to one or more of them consult the list on the WIPO website, which is updated regularly.[27]

- The Paris Convention
- The Berne Convention
- The International Convention for the Protection of Performers, Producers of Phonograms and Broadcasting Organizations (known as the Rome Convention)
- The WIPO Copyright Treaty
- The WIPO Performances and Phonograms Treaty
- The Beijing Treaty on Audio-visual Performances
- The Marrakesh Treaty to Facilitate Access to Published Works for Persons Who Are Blind, Visually Impaired or Otherwise Print Disabled
- The Brussels Convention Relating to the Distribution of Programme-Carrying Signals Transmitted by Satellite
- The Convention for the Protection of Producers of Phonograms Against Unauthorized Duplication of Their Phonograms (Geneva Phonograms Convention)
- The Madrid Agreement for the Repression of False and Deceptive Indications of Source on Goods

---

27 WIPO, "Members Profiles", www.wipo.int/wipolex/en/national.jsp, accessed 7 April 2015.

- The Nairobi Treaty on the Protection of the Olympic Symbol
- The Patent Law Treaty[28]
- The Trademark Law Treaty
- Singapore Treaty on the Law of Trademarks.

One should add to this a treaty administered at WIPO but technically by a separate secretariat, namely the International Union for the Protection of New Varieties of Plants.

We do not review each one of these agreements in detail, but it is important to bear in mind that in addition to the three major instruments discussed above (the Berne and Paris Conventions and the TRIPS Agreement), there are several others, smaller in scope, which may affect the analysis of any particular situation. We review the "big three", however, and provide an indication of the role of other instruments in context.

2.1   International intellectual property before the TRIPS Agreement

The Paris and Berne Conventions, which were initially negotiated in the 1880s and last revised on substance in the 1960s,[29] form the normative backbone of the international intellectual property system pre-TRIPS. The TRIPS Agreement changed the field of international intellectual property by including an effective enforcement mechanism. Much of its substance, however, is the inclusion by reference of instruments created long before TRIPS, in particular the Paris Convention and the Berne Convention.

2.1.1   The Paris Convention

The Paris Convention was first signed in 1883 and entered into force on 7 July 1884. It had two main objectives: (1) to extend to all member nations the principle of national treatment (in other words, the obligation to treat foreign nationals no less favourably than nationals); and (2) to guarantee minimum standards of protection for patents, industrial designs and trademarks.

---

28 Not to be confused with the *draft* Substantive Patent Law Treaty (SPLT) mentioned below.

29 Except for the Appendix added to the Berne Convention in 1971 – see Section [2.1.2].

As member countries increased their levels of protection and started to coordinate the evolution of their national laws, it became possible to increase the level of harmonization and to agree to rules designed to facilitate the acquisition of patent and trademark rights in foreign countries. These changes to the Convention were made at revision conferences held in various cities, all in Western Europe except for one conference held in Washington DC. The last such conference was held in Stockholm (Sweden) in 1967. This is referred to as the Stockholm Act of the Paris Convention. There have been no revisions since then, and it is unlikely that there will be due to the complex, unanimity-based process of revision conferences. Such consent among 176 countries (as of November 2015) on any issue is unlikely.

The Paris Convention is administered by WIPO. Because of the foreseen difficulty in revising the Convention, WIPO member states have adopted separate instruments, such as the Trademark Law Treaty (adopted in 1994) and the Patent Law Treaty (adopted in 2000), which are also procedural instruments. Although the Paris Convention is partly a procedural instrument, it contains several important substantive rules that are minimum substantive standards.

The Paris Convention contains four main sets of provisions:[30]

(1)   Rights and obligations of Paris Union members and establishment of the Union

- Article 6ter, which protects armorial bearings, flags and state emblems and those of intergovernmental organizations. The provision both prohibits the use and registration of trademarks consisting or containing official symbols and creates a registry administered by WIPO, of official symbols (without substantive examination). This register can be searched online.[31]
- Articles 12–24, which govern the administrative operation of the "Paris Union", in other words, the Union composed of all states party to the Convention. Article 12 obliges member states to create a national industrial property office.

---

30 A detailed analysis of the 1967 text of the Convention may be found in G. Bodenhausen, *Guide to the Paris Convention*, Geneva: BIRPI 1969.

31 WIPO IP Services, "Article 6ter Structured Search", www.wipo.int/ipdl/en/6ter/search-struct.jsp, accessed 9 April 2015.

- Articles 26–30, which govern the entry into force and revision of the Convention.

(2)   Requirements or authorization to legislate in certain areas[32]

In the area of patents:

- Article 4D, which provides a one-year time period to file foreign patent applications, thus allowing time for translation, paperwork, etc. This period, also known as the "right of priority", is also governed by Article 4.
- Article 4G(2), which concerns the division of "complex" patent applications into "divisional applications" while maintaining the original filing date.
- Article 5A, which concerns obligations to "work" a patent within a country, the possible abuse of patent rights and ways to remedy such abuse, including forfeiture (termination) of the patent and the issuance of a compulsory license. Those rules must now be read in conjunction with the obligations imposed by the TRIPS Agreement.
- Article 5*bis*(2), which allows members to restore patents which lapsed for failure to pay the required fees.

In the area of industrial designs:

- Article 5*quinquies*, which requires that industrial designs shall be protected in all countries. Some countries protect designs by patents others by copyright or a combination of both and others still have separate design systems (which can involve registered or unregistered rights).
- Article 5B, requires unlike patents, the protection for industrial design cannot be subject to forfeiture.

And in the area of trademarks:

- Article 6*bis*(2), which provides protection for well-known marks. This provision is discussed in greater detail below.

---

32 Such an authorization may not seem necessary. It is a basic principle of international law that States can do anything that is not unlawful. However, an authorization to act can (a) remove any doubt as to the legality of an act that could otherwise be seen as contrary to another provision of the Convention and/or (b) impose parameters for action.

- Article 6*septies*(3), dealing with agents.
- Article 10*bis*, which requires states to provide substantive protection against unfair competition. This provision is also discussed below.
- Article 10*ter*, which requires effective protection against false indications and other unlawful acts concerning trademarks and unfair competition.

And finally two general provisions, applicable to all forms of industrial property (trademarks, patents, utility models where national law so provides, such as the United States, and industrial designs):

- Article 11, which provides for temporary protection of industrial property rights in respect of goods exhibited at an international exhibition.
- Article 25, which contains a general obligation to give effect to the Convention in national law.

(3) Provisions regulating the substantive law of industrial property requiring the application of domestic laws

- Articles 2 and 3, which provide for national treatment (discussed below).
- Articles 9 and 10, which deal with remedies in the area of trademarks, including seizure (Article 9(3)). Such remedies are also applicable to false indications of source (Article 10(1)). Article 9 is discussed in greater detail below.

(4) Provisions regulating substantive law of industrial property regarding rights and obligations of private parties

These provisions may be directly applicable in the national law of certain countries.

General provisions:

- Article 1, which contains a definition of the objects of "industrial property".
- Article 5, which regulates the obligation to exploit (or "work") industrial property rights and the issuance of compulsory licenses.
- Article 5*bis*, which provides a grace period to pay applicable fees.

In the area of patent law:

- Article 4, which concerns the right of priority, namely a 12-month window to apply for a patent in countries other than the country of original application while maintaining the original filing date, which is relevant *inter alia* for the analysis of novelty of the purported invention.[33]
- Article 4*bis*, which provides that each (national) patent is independent of patents issued in other countries. This basically means that state A does not have to grant or invalidate a patent on an invention because state B did so, even if said patents result from the same application (using the priority date system just mentioned).
- Article 4*ter*, which provides inventors with the right to be mentioned in the patent. It can be seen as the equivalent of a moral right for inventors (see Article 6*bis*(1) of the Berne Convention).
- Article 4*quater*, which limits the member states' power to refuse or annul patents when the sale (not the manufacture[34]) of a product is restricted under national law.
- Article 5*ter*, which deals with patent infringement where a patented device forms part of a vessel, aircraft or "land vehicle".
- Article 5*quater*, which concerns process patents. A frequent issue with process patents is whether protection is available on products manufactured (legally) by the patented process when the product itself is not patented. Under this provision, if the product manufactured in state A and imported into state B is made using a process patented in state B, the patent owner shall have rights in state B with respect to such a product.[35]

In the area of trademarks:

- Article 6, which provides for the registration and independence of trademarks. This provision provides for the application of national law to the filing and registration of trademarks. However, it must be read together with Article 6*quinquies* (see below).

---

33 Under the Patent Cooperation Treaty (see Section [4.4.4]), this window is effectively now 30 months.

34 Cases where the manufacture of a product is illegal but its sale legal in the same territory are relatively rare. Under the Paris Convention, the status of the patent in such a case would be left to national law – although the principle of Article 4*quater* could still quite logically apply.

35 This provision must be read in conjunction with the TRIPS Agreement to offer a more complete picture.

- Article 6*ter*, which limits the right to register and use a trademark consisting or containing an official symbol or hallmark.
- Article 6*quater*, concerning the assignment of trademarks. The issue here is whether one can assign a trademark without the business (industrial or commercial establishment) or goodwill (essentially the circle of actual or potential customers that give the mark a reputation) to which the mark belongs. In certain countries, such an assignment may constitute abandonment of the mark, especially if the public is misled.
- Article 6*quinquies*, dealing with the registration of foreign trademarks. This is a very significant provision. It obliges all states party to the Paris Convention to accept a foreign mark duly registered in its country of origin for filing and protect it as is (*"telle quelle"*), that is, in the same form. This obligation is subject to a number of exceptions. First, the mark must be a mark in the country in which registration and/or protection is sought. A country that does not recognize olfactory (smell) marks, for example, would be under no obligation to change its laws. Second, a country may deny registration for three reasons: if the rights of a third party would be infringed (prior user); if the mark is devoid of distinctive character or is descriptive of the kind, quality, quantity purpose, value or origin of the goods or time or production or is a term customary in the current language (this may happen, for example, when people in states A and B use different languages); and finally if the mark would be contrary to morality or public order.
- Article 6*septies*, dealing with trademark agents. Several more recent instruments impact this area, including the Madrid System (Agreement and Protocol), the Trademark Law Treaty and the Singapore Treaty on the Law of Trademarks.
- Article 7, which provides for the exclusion of the nature of the goods as a bar to the registration of a mark.
- Article 8, which protects trade names. These are often the names of businesses not used as marks. For example, company ABC (name) may be selling product XYZ (mark).
- Article 10(2), which deals with false indications of source and provides an interest in pursuing same.
- Article 10*bis*(2) and (3), which define acts of unfair competition and provide rights in respect thereof (see below).

It should be noted that while the scope of the Paris Convention appears quite broad, the language used provides significant flexibility to the member states. In addition, while Article 28 theoretically provides for recourse to the International Court of Justice in case of a dispute (provided parties have agreed to the Court's jurisdiction), this mechanism has never been used. This means that in practice member states cannot legally force other members to implement the Paris Convention (unlike the TRIPS Agreement). They can, however, legally force parties to comply with the parts of the Paris Convention incorporated into TRIPS via the WTO dispute settlement system.

Three examples taken from the trademark-related provisions of the Paris Convention will suffice to show the normative weakness (relative to the TRIPS Agreement) of many provisions of this instrument. As the following examples demonstrate, this weakness often results from the self-judging nature of compliance with a country's obligations.

Article 6*bis*
(1) The countries of the Union undertake, ... to refuse or to cancel the registration, and to prohibit the use, of a trademark which constitutes a reproduction, an imitation, or a translation, liable to create confusion, *of a mark considered by the competent authority of the country of registration or use to be well known in that country* as being already the mark of a person entitled to the benefits of this Convention and *used for identical or similar goods*. These provisions shall also apply when the essential part of the mark constitutes a reproduction of any such well-known mark or an imitation liable to create confusion therewith. (Emphasis added.)

Article 7*bis*
(1) The countries of the Union undertake to accept for filing and to protect *collective marks* belonging to associations the existence of which is not contrary to the law of the country of origin, even if such associations do not possess an industrial or commercial establishment.
(2) *Each country shall be the judge* of the particular conditions under which a collective mark shall be protected and may refuse protection if the mark is contrary to the public interest. (Emphasis added.)

Finally, Article 9, which seems not to contain any enforceable obligation, provides:

Article 9
(1) All goods unlawfully bearing a trademark or trade name shall be *seized* on importation into those countries of the Union where such mark or trade name is entitled to legal protection.

(2) Seizure shall likewise be effected in the country where the unlawful affixation occurred or in the country into which the goods were imported.
. . .
(5) If the legislation of a country *does not permit seizure on importation*, seizure shall be replaced by prohibition of importation or by seizure inside the country.
(6) If the legislation of a country permits *neither seizure on importation nor prohibition of importation nor seizure inside the country*, then, until such time as the legislation is modified accordingly, these measures shall be replaced by the actions and remedies available in such cases to nationals under the law of such country. (Emphasis added.)

This means that the enforceable obligational content of Article 9 is extremely limited. By contrast, a number of other provisions do have normative teeth.

Article 5(4) of the Paris Convention on compulsory patent licenses, for example, is quite specific:

A compulsory license may not be applied for on the ground of failure to work or insufficient working before the expiration of a period of four years from the date of filing of the patent application or three years from the date of the grant of the patent, whichever period expires last; it shall be refused if the patentee justifies his inaction by legitimate reasons. Such a compulsory license shall be non-exclusive and shall not be transferable, even in the form of the grant of a sub-license, except with that part of the enterprise or goodwill which exploits such license.

The same could be said of Article 10*bis*(2) and (3) of the Paris Convention:

Article10*bis*
(2) Any act of competition contrary to honest practices in industrial or commercial matters constitutes an act of unfair competition.
(3) The following in particular shall be prohibited:
  (i)   all acts of such a nature as to create confusion by any means whatever with the establishment, the goods, or the industrial or commercial activities, of a competitor;
  (ii) false allegations in the course of trade of such a nature as to discredit the establishment, the goods, or the industrial or commercial activities, of a competitor;
  (iii) indications or allegations the use of which in the course of trade

is liable to mislead the public as to the nature, the manufacturing process, the characteristics, the suitability for their purpose, or the quantity, of the goods.

In addition to the weakness of some of the rights it does provide, there are significant gaps in the Paris Convention. Among the most notable omissions are:

- a term of protection for any of the rights and obligations;
- the definition of patentability criteria;
- the extent of patent rights;
- conditions surrounding the issuance of compulsory licenses;
- rules governing the examination of trademark applications;
- protection of service marks (as marks); and
- material rules on ownership and enforcement.

2.1.2   The Berne Convention

The Convention signed at Berne, Switzerland in September 1886 is the copyright equivalent of the Paris Convention. Like the Paris Convention, it established the principle of national treatment (discussed below) in the area of copyright and began a process of gradual harmonization of minimum standards to be enacted in national copyright laws, which continued at the six revision conferences of that Convention. The last substantive revision happened at the same time as the revision of the Paris Convention, in Stockholm in 1967. However, an Appendix was added in Paris four years later in the wake of the massive wave of decolonization that started in the late 1950s. The Appendix allows developing countries to issue compulsory translation and reproduction licenses for books under certain conditions. The last Act is thus referenced as the (1971) "Paris Act" of the Berne Convention – not to be confused with the Paris Convention. For the reasons explained above with respect to the Paris Convention, it is unlikely that a new act or version of the Berne Convention will ever be adopted. This would require unanimous consent from its 168 member countries (as of 1 November 2015). However, as we will see below, two new conventions were adopted under the aegis of WIPO in December 1996 that may be seen as adding to the Berne Convention, although they are stand-alone instruments.

The Berne Convention has a different structure from the Paris Convention. The Berne Convention contains essentially two types of provisions, namely those of a substantive nature and those concerning the administration of the Berne Union, in other words, the Union composed of all countries party to the Convention. Here is a quick glance at the Convention's content:[36]

First, the Convention contains a number of general provisions:

- Article 2 indirectly defines the expression "literary and artistic works" by providing a list of categories of the types of works that should be protected. And artistic is used to include dramatic and musical works and other categories. It also allows member countries to require fixation; protect translations, adaptations, arrangements, and collections (compilations); and exclude or limit the copyright protection of official texts (as is the case in the United States), news and works of applied arts.
- Article 2*bis* allows limitations on the protection of political and "legal" speeches.
- Articles 3 and 4 define the so-called "attachment factors" according to which the protection of foreign works under the Convention is based, such as the nationality of author or the place of publication of work.
- Article 5 provides for national treatment.
- Article 6 provides that a member may limit the protection of nationals of another member that does not adequately protect its own authors.
- Article 6*bis* protects the moral rights of integrity and authorship.
- Articles 7 and 7*bis* provide a term of protection, which in most cases is the life of the author plus 50 years. In a derogation to national treatment principles, states that opt for a longer term may limit the protection of works from a state in which the term is shorter to that shorter term (in other words, application of the term in the country or origin).

The Convention also contains a number of general provisions, including a provision on ownership of cinematographic (audio-visual) works (Article 14*bis*); the enforcement of copyright (Article 15), including seizure of infringing copies (Article 16); and provisions allowing member states to make other bilateral agreements to increase the

---

36 A more complete explanation may be found in M. Ficsor, *Guide to the Copyright and Related Rights Treaties Administered by WIPO and Glossary of Copyright and Related Rights Terms*, Geneva: WIPO 2004; S. Ricketson and J. C. Ginsburg, *International Copyright and Neighboring Rights: The Berne Convention and Beyond*, Oxford: Oxford University Press, 2006.

level of protection guaranteed by the Convention (Articles 19 and 20). Finally, the protection of works in existence at the time a country joins the Convention is governed by Article 18.

The Convention then provides the economic rights that form part of the Convention's copyright "bundle":

- The right of reproduction (Article 9).
- The right of translation (Articles 8, 11, and 11*ter*) and the right of adaptation (Articles 12 and 14).
- The right of public performance and communication to the public (Articles 11 and 11*bis*).
- The right of "public recitation" and communication to the public of a recitation (Article 11*ter*).
- The "*droit de suite*" or right to obtain a share on the resale of a work of art (Article 14*ter*), which is optional under the Convention (a country may decide to provide such a right and if it does so it can provide the right on the basis of reciprocity (that is, to countries that also provide the right) rather than on the normal national treatment basis).

The Convention also permits certain exceptions:

- Quotations and illustrations used for teaching (Article 10).
- Reproduction by the press, the broadcasting or the communication to the public by wire of articles published in newspapers or periodicals on current economic, political or religious topics, and of broadcast works of the same character (Article 10*bis*).
- Compulsory licensing for broadcasting and retransmission (Article 11*bis*(2)).
- Compulsory licensing for the reproduction of musical works on sound recordings (Article 13).

Articles 1 and 22–38 are of an administrative nature and will not be discussed here.[37]

---

37 Article 1 has a dual nature. While mostly administrative in that its purpose is to "establish" the Union, it is also substantive in that it states the purpose of the Union, namely to "protect the rights of authors in their literary and artistic works". Article 37(3) is also relevant: it provides that in case of discrepancy, the French version of the Convention prevails. The Convention also contains an Appendix with special provisions for developing countries. It is seldom used and will not be discussed further here.

Because the Convention was last revised before the massive use of personal computers, digital carriers for music and images (for example, CDs, DVDs, MP3 players, and the like), and the Internet, a number of countries felt that the norms had to be updated. Part of that update was effected by the 1994 TRIPS Agreement (see below), while the two WIPO Treaties of 1996 (see below) were adopted to adapt the international copyright framework to the Internet.

While WIPO continued its efforts to develop new intellectual property norms, the process was greatly decelerated between 1986 and April 1994, while more or less the same countries were negotiating intellectual property norms in a different forum, the future WTO. On 15 April 1994, most WIPO members signed the Agreement Establishing the WTO, including the TRIPS Agreement.

2.2   The emergence of the TRIPS Agreement

Internationally, the instrument that has had the most dramatic impact on international intellectual property rules is the TRIPS Agreement. As mentioned above, the TRIPS Agreement is Annex 1C of the Agreement Establishing the WTO, which was signed at Marrakesh on 15 April 1994 and entered into force on 1 January 1995. The agreement provided that no country had to comply with its provisions for one year after it came into force.[38] In addition there were delayed periods for compliance with some provisions for developing countries, and least developed countries have had further extension before compliance is required. On 6 November 2015, the TRIPS Council extended this further until 1 January 2033 – unless a particular country ceases to be in the least developed category if that happens before 2021.[39] As of October 2015, additional extensions were under consideration in the Council for TRIPS.

The TRIPS Agreement provides for minimum standards of intellectual property protection in relation to copyright, trademarks, patents, GIs, industrial designs, layout designs, confidential information,

---

38 TRIPS Agreement, Article 65(1).

39 TRIPS Agreement, Articles 65–66 and details of agreement and negotiations over subsequent extensions are available on the WTO website. See Extension of the Transition Period under Article 66.1 for Least Developed Country Members – Decision of the Council for TRIPS of 6 November 2015. WTO document IP/C/73.

and prevention of some anti-competitive licensing practices. It also requires that countries provide for the enforcement of intellectual property rights by or before national courts, administrative agencies and customs authorities. WTO members are required to enact intellectual property laws at the national level or otherwise comply with those minimum standards. Members may provide more extensive protection than the minimum standards dictate, and the mode of implementation at national level is a matter for each member to determine.[40] This allows for a significant degree of national autonomy over implementation, resulting in different laws in different WTO members. To ensure that these different laws do not result in discrimination against members of the TRIPS Agreement, the cornerstone of the Agreement, as with most other intellectual property agreements, is the principle of national treatment. Additionally, in the TRIPS Agreement national treatment is accompanied by the most-favoured nation (MFN) principle. To demonstrate these principles practically, their use in the TRIPS Agreement is discussed below.

Besides the TRIPS Agreement there is a range of agreements relating to specific areas of intellectual property. As was mentioned above, unlike those other agreements, TRIPS falls under the purview of the WTO, and so the TRIPS Agreement brings with it the WTO dispute settlement mechanism. Previous international agreements in the field have lacked such mechanisms. This is one of the achievements of the TRIPS Agreement.[41]

As mentioned above, the TRIPS Agreement is the most extensive and influential international agreement concerning intellectual property. Understanding the history, logic, and general principles of the TRIPS Agreement will help set the ground work for grasping the current state of international intellectual property. The most impactful part of TRIPS, the dispute settlement mechanism, is also described in this section.

---

40 TRIPS Agreement, Article 1(1), provides that "Members shall give effect to the provisions of this Agreement. Members may, but shall not be obliged to, implement in their law more extensive protection than is required by this Agreement, provided that such protection does not contravene the provisions of this Agreement. Members shall be free to determine the appropriate method of implementing the provisions of this Agreement within their own legal system and practice."

41 R. C. Dreyfuss and A. F. Lowenfeld, "Two Achievements of the Uruguay Round: Putting TRIPS and Dispute Settlement Together", 37 *Virginia Journal of International Law* (1997), 275.

2.2.1   The TRIPS Agreement negotiations

The TRIPS Agreement, together with the 1967 Stockholm Conference that adopted the revised Berne and Paris Conventions and created WIPO, the substantive parts of which are incorporated into TRIPS, was the most significant milestone in the development of intellectual property in the twentieth century. Its scope was much broader than that of any previous international agreement, covering not only all areas already (sometimes only partly) protected under previous agreements, but also giving new life to treaties that had not been wholly successful (such as the Rome Convention) and protecting for the first time rights that did not benefit from any multilateral protection. In addition, and some right holders would say perhaps more importantly than its broad substantive coverage, the TRIPS Agreement enshrined detailed rules on one of the most difficult and, for some, painful aspects of intellectual property rights: enforcement. It also subjected the whole agreement to dispute resolution.

In 1986, members of the GATT, the predecessor of the WTO, launched the "Uruguay Round of Multilateral Trade Negotiations" at Punta del Este (Uruguay). The Declaration that launched the Round, which ended at a meeting in Marrakesh in April 1994, after a number of near failures, contained the following negotiating mandate in respect of intellectual property:

> In order to reduce the distortions and impediments to international trade, and taking into account the need to promote effective and adequate protection of intellectual property rights, and to ensure that measures and procedures to enforce intellectual property rights do not themselves become barriers to legitimate trade, the negotiations shall aim to clarify GATT provisions and elaborate as appropriate new rules and disciplines.

> Negotiations shall aim to develop a multilateral framework of principles, rules and disciplines dealing with international trade in counterfeit goods, taking into account work already undertaken in GATT.

> These negotiations shall be without prejudice to other complementary initiatives that may be taken in the World Intellectual Property Organization and elsewhere to deal with these matters.[42]

In comparing this text with the TRIPS Agreement, the work accomplished between Punta del Este and Marrakesh becomes readily

---

42 GATT Document, Ministerial Declaration on the Uruguay Round of 20 September 1986, pp. 7–8.

apparent. The TRIPS Agreement is the broadest and most extensive multilateral agreement in the field of intellectual property, covering the entire area and adding enforcement, acquisition, and MFN obligations to new and existing rules and incorporating those rules in what could be considered the only truly effective and binding dispute settlement mechanism between states. That this was negotiated at multilateral level on the basis of a limited initial mandate one could say is rather amazing.

The negotiations were difficult for many reasons, including the fact that the GATT secretariat and many, if not most, of the negotiators, in particular those from developing countries, had little if any expertise in intellectual property.

The playing field was clearly delineated. Industrialized countries had their vision of the basic parameters and scope of a future TRIPS Agreement. A number of key issues divided their proposals, however, and later entered the list of so-called "North–North" issues to be resolved. Other proposals targeted mostly developing countries and their reaction made it abundantly clear that the negotiations would not be easy.

Most of the initial North–North issues remained unsettled in the final agreement.[43] Many of the developing countries' proposals were all but forgotten, except for two Articles that were supposed to reflect their concerns, namely Articles 7 and 8 and a few preambular provisions. Developing countries were basically just given more time to implement the TRIPS Agreement than that given to developed countries.

The timing of the implementation of TRIPS is relatively complicated because of the various types of countries involved. The TRIPS Agreement was formally adopted as Annex 1C of the Final Act Embodying the Results of the Uruguay Round of Multilateral Trade Negotiations, at Marrakesh on 15 April 1994. It entered into force on 1 January 1995. Article 64 of the Agreement provided for a general transition period of one year. The Agreement entered into force with respect to the more industrialized WTO members on 1 January 1996. The Agreement entered into force with respect to the developing

---

43 This included at the time issues such as the level of protection of biotechnological inventions, the protection of geographical indications for wines and spirits, and national treatment provisions on private copying levies.

countries as of 1 January 2000, although these members could delay the protection by patents of product inventions in "areas of technology not so protectable [(in other words, by patent)] in its territory" (such as pharmaceuticals) until 1 January 2005, subject to the other provisions of TRIPS (for example, on national treatment, MFN, enforcement and acquisition of rights) and to the "mailbox" protection provisions of Article 70.8 and the obligation to provide "exclusive marketing rights" contained in Article 70.9. Least developed WTO members benefited from a transitional period that gave them until 1 January 2006 to apply the Agreement (except for a few provisions, especially national treatment), with possible extensions by the TRIPS Council. Such an extension (until 2033) on the introduction of patent protection for pharmaceutical products was granted to least developed WTO members at the Doha (Qatar) Ministerial Conference in November 2015.

2.2.2 Post-TRIPS negotiations

At the Doha Conference, which followed a very public failure of the Conference held the prior year in Seattle, a new Round was launched. The Ministerial Declaration contains very few provisions dealing with intellectual property. It calls on members to complete negotiations on the Uruguay Round's unfinished business (many of the North–North issues, including the protection of GIs). In regard to intellectual property, the language of the Doha Declaration is a measure of the sea change since 1994.[44] In the three paragraphs concerning the TRIPS Agreement, there are scant opportunities for demands of increased intellectual property protection and greater recognition of developing country interests. Paragraph 17 states that TRIPS should be implemented "in a manner supportive of public health, by promoting both access to existing medicines and research and development into new medicines and, in this connection, are adopting a separate declaration". In the following paragraph, the Doha Declaration addresses a mostly North–North issue, the completion of the negotiations on GIs on wines and spirits. Paragraph 19, which is perhaps the most famous of the Declaration, instructs the TRIPS Council to:

> examine, *inter alia*, the relationship between the TRIPS Agreement and the *Convention on Biological Diversity*, the protection of traditional knowledge and folklore, and other relevant new developments raised by members

---

44 WTO, Ministerial Declaration, 14 November 2001, www.wto.org/english/thewtoe/min01e/mindecle.htm, accessed 7 April 2015 (hereinafter Doha Declaration).

pursuant to Article 71.1. In undertaking this work, the TRIPS Council shall be guided by the objectives and principles set out in Articles 7 and 8 of the TRIPS Agreement and shall take fully into account the development dimension.

In other words, apart from the possible increase in protection of names of wines and spirits as a result of negotiations on a multilateral register foreseen in the second paragraph, the Doha Declaration essentially reflects the concerns of developing countries. The first paragraph insists on the balance between the need for access to intellectual property and its protection. It may serve as a philosophical underpinning for ongoing discussions.

The third paragraph is, however, the most significant for at least two main reasons. First, together with the separate Declaration on the TRIPS Agreement and Public Health that was also adopted at Doha, it led to the adoption of a Decision of the WTO General Council on 30 August 2003 on Implementation of paragraph 6 of the Doha Declaration on the TRIPS Agreement and Public Health (the so-called "Paragraph-6 system"). This Decision allows, under certain conditions, WTO members to export generic versions of drugs used to treat diseases such as HIV to countries that can neither afford nor manufacture these pharmaceuticals.

The third paragraph is also important because of its mention of the CBD.[45] The CBD, signed ratified or approved by 196 countries as of 1 November 2015, is important not because of its normative content, which is rather weak in the areas that overlap with the TRIPS Agreement, but rather because it opened the door to the inclusion of TRIPS in a broader normative framework. The most often-mentioned provision of the CBD in its relations with TRIPS is Article 8(j) concerning in-situ conservation. This Article reads as follows:

> Each Contracting Party shall, *as far as possible* and *as appropriate*:
> (j) *Subject to its national legislation*, respect, preserve and maintain knowledge, innovations and practices of indigenous and local communities embodying traditional lifestyles relevant for the conservation and sustainable use of biological diversity and promote their wider application

---

45 United Nations, "The Rio de Janeiro Convention on Biological Diversity", 14 June 1992, 31 I.L.M. 818, (entered in force 29 December 1993), at www.cbd.int/doc/legal/cbd-en.pdf, accessed 2 September 2015 (hereinafter CBD).

> with the approval and involvement of the holders of such knowledge, innovations and practices and encourage the equitable sharing of the benefits arising from the utilization of such knowledge, innovations and practices. (Emphasis added.)

In spite of the numerous "outs", the CBD remains important in the Doha context in its insistence on the need to bring holders of traditional knowledge into the picture of international intellectual property. This is reinforced by the specific mention of traditional knowledge and folklore in the Doha Declaration. Traditional knowledge is discussed further later in this book.

The WTO Director-General's report of 9 June 2008 summarized the state of play on the issue of the relationship between the TRIPS Agreement and the CBD and the protection of traditional knowledge and folklore:

> There is important common ground on key underlying objectives, notably the importance of the TRIPS Agreement and the CBD being implemented in a mutually supportive way, the avoidance of erroneous patents for inventions that involve the use of genetic resources and related traditional knowledge and securing compliance with national access and benefit-sharing regimes. Moreover, there is wide acceptance of the need for patent offices to have available to them the information necessary to make proper decisions on the grant of patents and to avoid any undermining of the role of the patent system in providing incentives for innovation.[46]

The changing face of international intellectual property is also evidenced by the reference in the Doha Declaration to Articles 7 and 8 of the TRIPS Agreement, which were the two provisions inserted originally to reflect the concerns of developing countries. Though they have been given little regard up until now in dispute settlement proceedings in the WTO (see Section [3.2] [Principles of Treaty Interpretation section]), these two provisions could be given a somewhat higher normative profile in future disputes because of what is a possible "special status" in the Doha text. Article 7 is cut from the same tree as paragraph 17 of the Doha Declaration (in other words, the first of the three dealing with the TRIPS Agreement). It reads as follows:

---

46 WTO Director-General's Report, 9 June 2008,WT/GC/W/591, [5], at www.wto.org/english/ tratop_e/trips_e/giextension_cbd_dgreport_9juno8_e.pdf, accessed 22 September 2015.

The protection and enforcement of intellectual property rights should contribute to the promotion of technological innovation and to the transfer
and dissemination of technology, to the mutual advantage of producers and
users of technological knowledge and in a manner conducive to social and
economic welfare, and to a balance of rights and obligations.

Many people in industrialized countries have voiced a similar concern as those from developing countries. Many argue that it is wrong
to think that, in all cases, more intellectual property protection is
necessarily better. There is an increasing recognition that, while
intellectual property is necessary at least in certain areas to justify
enormous research and development expenditure (some pharmaceutical patents are a good example), there are competing concerns
and particularly competing public goods relating to health, culture
and information and related access in particular. Consequently, the
optimal configuration of intellectual property norms could not be
ascertained on the basis of available empirical data. The pre-TRIPS
historical development of norms was a haphazard process and does
not offer sufficient economic, social, or philosophical justifications for continuing along the same path without further analysis.
Post-TRIPS there is more better data and evidence. Although what
amounts to the optimal configuration of norms remains a hotly contested topic. In parallel, many countries argue that major industrialized countries only adopted high protection norms *after* they had
developed economically.[47] They also argue that many "free*r*-trade"
(emphasis added) measures that industrialized countries demand
relate to goods with a high ideational or informational content, areas
in which it is often harder for smaller or developing economies to
compete. At the same time, trade barriers are maintained on goods
with which they could compete, such as agricultural products and
textile products.

All this is now reinforced by views emerging within industrialized
countries not only about the possible negative impact of imposing too-
high protection norms on developing countries but also on the development of a vibrant technological and creative culture. One can point

---

47 This is, roughly, the debate between the Development theorists (according to whom development
    will follow the putting in place of a normative framework as well as a judicial and administrative
    infrastructure that mirrors those of industrialized nations) and the Dependency theorists, who
    argue that adopting those high-protection standards in developing countries will lead to increased
    economic dependency of those countries.

to movements such as open source software, Creative Commons in the field of copyright and to analyses of the sometimes poor social value of letting only the market dictate the path of innovation. Indeed, leaving it entirely to the market by giving strong exclusive rights to market-driven innovation may mean more money to fight baldness or erectile difficulties than tropical or orphan diseases. Companies decide, unsurprisingly given legal and economic structures, based on how they can maximize profit, not on the societal value of their investments. This also means that countries may be tempted to "socially engineer" their intellectual property regime.

2.3 The structure of the TRIPS Agreement

The TRIPS negotiators had a choice. They could have tried to reinvent the intellectual property wheel and in some cases tried to do so. For example, detailed provisions on the protection of layout designs of integrated circuits were tabled in 1990. In theory one could perhaps replace existing forms of protection with more economically efficient ones. This would have had advantages, of course, at least from a theoretical point of view: redesigning the protection from scratch, unencumbered by previous rules and practices. But the disadvantages far outweighed any possible gains. Some of the world's largest industries (pharmaceutical, agri-food, computer software, entertainment, luxury goods) depend on effective protection of their intellectual property rights. This does not mean that the system cannot be revisited or indeed key aspects of it changed. Indeed, this has become a necessity in many areas. In copyright, an example is where the survival of authors is in question as many of them cannot get paid. In patent law access to medicines issues continue.

Moreover, each and every legitimate business relies in part on intellectual property to flourish, if only because its name or trademark is protected. A complete change of the intellectual property framework could have wreaked havoc in forcing each company to adapt. The transition cost would have been enormous. Industries, inventors, creators, policy makers, courts, administrative, and enforcement authorities probably would have had to make unreasonable efforts to understand and apply the new forms of protection. TRIPS negotiators were thus wise to opt for an updating of existing rules. Looking at the Paris Convention, the Berne Convention, the Rome Convention, and the Treaty on Intellectual Property in Respect of Integrated Circuits (which never entered into force), TRIPS negotiators came to the following conclusions:

- Few rights had to be created anew, as those conventions offered a very good basis and in most cases relied on decades of recognized practices; however, in respect of many existing rights, binding clarifications were required. In addition, some new rights were necessary (for example, a rental right in copyright and rights in respect of GIs).
- Some of the exceptions and limitations contained in those existing conventions were no longer necessary or justified.
- Provisions on enforcement had to be added to address one of the main inadequacies of existing conventions.
- There was a need for a binding dispute settlement mechanism in the field of intellectual property.
- Some additional specific rules would be useful, such as the application of the MFN principle, rules facilitating acquisition procedures and transparency requirements with regard to laws, rules and other practices.

Based on these conclusions, negotiators used existing conventions as a logical point of departure. As a first step, they looked at each one and decided which provisions should be incorporated into the future TRIPS Agreement. All of the substantive provisions of the Paris and Berne Conventions (with the exception of Article 6*bis* of the latter) and the Washington Treaty[48] (with the exception of a provision on compulsory licenses) were thus incorporated by reference and are enforceable at the WTO. The second step was to add the necessary new rights, seen in the addition of provisions on rental rights, GIs, trademarks, and service marks, and on the protection of confidential information, although this latter issue is presented as a simple extension of existing obligations in respect of unfair competition. However, all the above provisions cover a fairly small part of the TRIPS Agreement as such. In fact, most of the provisions in Parts I and II of TRIPS either clarify existing obligations (sometimes increasing the level of protection) or restrict the possibility of using limitations or exceptions.

Once this had been achieved, the standards were in place. Negotiators, continued along the same path, and added an entirely new set of rules

---

48 Treaty on Intellectual Property in Respect of Integrated Circuits, adopted at Washington, DC, 26 May 1989.

on enforcement. There was no precedent for this in the field of intellectual property at the multilateral level. Provisions were thus drafted on the basis of concerns expressed by industry experts and other interested parties.

The final pieces of the puzzle could then be added, including more precise rules on acquisition and, more importantly, provisions bringing the TRIPS Agreement under the general WTO dispute settlement umbrella, known as the integrated dispute settlement system. And when the usual provisions on entry into force, including protection of existing subject matter and transitional periods on institutional arrangements were added the TRIPS Agreement was complete.

The TRIPS Agreement is part of the WTO system, which in turn cannot be read in "clinical isolation" from international legal principles, to use a phrase coined by the WTO Appellate Body. One of the important challenges of the Appellate Body and panels has been to develop the interface between TRIPS and non-WTO instruments, as discussed below in Section [3.2] [section about treaty interpretation and the relevance of other international agreements]. The extent to which external (non-WTO) norms are used to interpret TRIPS provisions is an evolving process. It should be informed by consensus reached in the TRIPS Council, relevant Declarations, such as the Doha Declaration, and the avoidance of non-negotiated changes or concessions.

2.4   General objectives of the TRIPS Agreement

Most international treaties in the field of intellectual property state some kind of purpose or objective in the preamble. The TRIPS Agreement preamble includes some important statements, which include the recognition of the link between intellectual property and trade, that intellectual property rights are private rights, and "[r]ecognizing the underlying public policy objectives of national systems for the protection of intellectual property, including developmental and technological objectives". In addition to the preamble the TRIPS Agreement contains two articles that deal with objectives and principles. These articles, which were mentioned above, are:

Article 7 *Objectives*
The protection and enforcement of intellectual property rights should contribute to the promotion of technological innovation and to the transfer

and dissemination of technology, to the mutual advantage of producers and users of technological knowledge and in a manner conducive to social and economic welfare, and to a balance of rights and obligations.

Article 8 *Principles*

(1)   Members may, in formulating or amending their laws and regulations, adopt measures necessary to protect public health and nutrition, and to promote the public interest in sectors of vital importance to their socio-economic and technological development, provided that such measures are consistent with the provisions of this Agreement.

(2)   Appropriate measures, provided that they are consistent with the provisions of this Agreement, may be needed to prevent the abuse of intellectual property rights by right holders or the resort to practices which unreasonably restrain trade or adversely affect the international transfer of technology.

In a dispute settlement procedure the widely worded objectives and principles of the TRIPS Agreement should assist in the interpretation of its provisions.[49] As noted above, in 2002 the WTO Declaration on the TRIPS Agreement and Public Heath emphasized the importance of Articles 7 and 8 in the interpretation of the TRIPS Agreement.[50]

As discussed, the TRIPS Agreement is an integral part of the law of the WTO. It stands alongside the main agreements on goods and services, GATT and the General Agreement on Trade in Services (GATS)[51] in the WTO covered agreements package, called a single undertaking.[52] At the time of the TRIPS Agreement negotiations there was much debate over the role of intellectual property in the world trade arena and since the creation of the TRIPS Agreement that debate has evolved. Even though some still dispute the wisdom of the explicit link between trade and intellectual property the link is well and truly established. It has always been there, but TRIPS certainly brought that to a new level. Today's debates are about bringing more "balance" or equilibrium into the substantive norms of intellectual property to reflect

---

49 TRIPS Agreement, Article 31. For a discussion of the interpretation of these provisions at the WTO; see S. Frankel, "The WTO's Application of 'the Customary Rules of Interpretation of Public International Law' to Intellectual Property", 46 *Virginia Journal of International Law* (2006), 365.

50 See Doha Declaration [5.a].

51 WTO, General Agreement on Trade in Services, WTO Agreement, Annex 1B (hereinafter GATS).

52 "Covered agreements" refers to those agreement covered by the Formation of the World Trade Organization.

the interests of the multiple actors involved in the global creation, dissemination and use of intellectual property. This has meant that intellectual property is discussed in many international fora. In addition, there are many free trade agreements (FTAs, discussed below), which increase the extent of and scope of intellectual property rights, and have frequently decreased the flexibility that the TRIPS Agreement allows national regimes and reduced the possibility of exceptions. In addition to FTAs, we also now see intellectual property being treated as an asset in investment agreements (this phenomenon is also discussed in Section 5.7 below).

It is useful here to consider the linkages between intellectual property and trade, which historically fell into two broad categories. The first category is through selling or licensing intellectual property rights in other territories. The second category is where the owner exports products or services embodying its intellectual property rights to a foreign territory. In both of these categories the rights owner must rely on local intellectual property laws. There are of course many variables between and within these two categories; an owner could adopt the first method in one territory and the second in another. The two groupings have formed the possible ways in which intellectual property rights fall into the channels of international trade. Both methods of protecting intellectual property rights have been features of international intellectual property law in one way or another for some time. The Internet as a method of distribution has added to this.

The bringing together of the trade regime with intellectual property creates some difficulties because the justifications behind national intellectual property laws, particularly the encouragement of creative and innovative works, are not always the same as those in the trade arena. The differences between trade in tangibles (free movement of goods) and trade in certain intangibles (territorial intellectual property protection) can also be lead to fundamentally different approaches to competition law. These differences underpin some of the conflicts that are prevalent in the systems today. For example, it is precisely because of the relationship between physical and intangible rights that issues around parallel importing of intellectual property goods have been so divisive and complex at international level. We discuss parallel importing in detail in Section 5.3.

The status of the TRIPS Agreement as a covered agreement in the WTO has the effect of recognizing intellectual property, within certain agreed limits, as an acceptable trade-related barrier. The significance of the trade barriers that intellectual property can create is that over-protecting intellectual property can be an inhibitor to the free flow of technology and the progress of science and innovation globally. If in practice real barriers were created, then neither the objectives of intellectual property law nor international trade would be met. In sum, over-protecting intellectual property does not achieve the barrier-lowering objectives of international trade, but can in fact inhibit it. As noted above, the TRIPS Agreement in its preamble makes it clear that it should be read in a way that is consistent with "GATT-style" liberalized trade. Any other interpretation would be at odds with the WTO context. We discuss interpretation in more detail in Section 3.2.

3 Key concepts of international intellectual property

3.1 The territorial nature of intellectual property

The legal rules of intellectual property rights are national or territorial. This contrasts with the global nature of trade in intellectual property and in the goods and services to which intellectual property relates.

"Territorial" has many meanings and effects in intellectual property law. First, it means that the rights are limited to the territory in which they are granted. A trademark or patent registered in one country, gives protection in that country and not in other countries. Protection in other countries for registered rights (patents, trademarks and sometimes designs) requires registration in those other countries. The territoriality principle applies even where rights, most significantly copyright, are not subject to mandatory registration. Copyright owners own a different copyright in each jurisdiction. What instruments like the Berne and Paris Conventions and the TRIPS Agreement have done is to impose minimum substantive standards, which each country can implement in different ways. When minimum standards and voluntary exceptions are combined with territoriality, significant variations are found between national laws.

The territoriality of intellectual property also allows owners to segment markets. This segmentation enables the charging of different prices and separate markets may have products of differing quality in each of those markets if the intellectual property owner so wishes. As we discuss further below, this market segmentation is preserved in countries that do not not allow parallel imports, while other countries which do allow parallel imports treat the world as one market, at least for some purposes.

This territorial nature of intellectual property rights also applies to enforcement. The setting of international intellectual property minimum standards arises from international agreements, which are instruments of public international law. The TRIPS Agreement requires that its members provide for minimum standards of enforcement, but it does not have rules about which courts can have jurisdiction over intellectual property disputes involving parties from two or more different countries or what law a court should apply in such disputes. These aspects of enforcement (jurisdiction and choice of law) are determined by rules of private international law, which are predominantly national and sometimes regional rules. Although, as we discuss below, there are some attempts internationally to reach agreement over private international law rules in intellectual property.

As they are national laws, and particularly as there is little international agreement about them, private international law rules vary between countries. In many jurisdictions if the validity of a registered right (such as a patent or a trademark) is contested then only the court in the territory that granted that right can hear any claim about the validity of the right.[53] Infringement can be a different matter. Some courts will hear foreign infringement claims and others will not. The complications come when validity is raised as a defence to infringement. Most often in that situation only the court in the territory where the right was granted can hear the dispute. For a long time the same territorial principle applied to infringement of copyright, but now some courts will hear infringement of copyright cases even if the infringement is not in or not only in its territory and even if the existence of copyright is contested. When a court decides that it has jurisdiction to hear a case the law applicable to the case may be an issue. Courts often like to apply their own law. Sometimes they apply foreign law, however.

The Berne Convention illustrates some of the complexities of private international law and the territoriality of intellectual property. Article 5(2) provides in part: "the extent of protection, as well as the means of redress afforded to the author to protect his rights, shall be governed exclusively by the laws of the country where protection is claimed".[54] A question is which country is the "country where protection is claimed"? Generally, the law that applies to an infringement is the law of the country where the infringement took place (the *lex loci*

---

53 See generally EC Council Regulation No 44/2001 of 22 December 2000 on jurisdiction and the recognition and enforcement of judgments in civil and commercial matters. Official Journal of the European Communities (L-12): 1–23, 2001 and *Potter v Broken Hill Pty Co Ltd* (1906) 3 CLR 479 (HCA).

54 Berne Convention, Article 5(2).

delicti). This will often, though not always, be the law of the country or region in which the court hearing the case is located (the *lex fori*). The Berne Convention does not contain a general choice of law rule, but contains a specific choice of law rule, Article 14*bis*(2)(a), which provides that copyright ownership in cinematographic works "shall be a matter for legislation in the country where protection is claimed". There are no agreements providing for choice of law rules in other areas of intellectual property.

During the 1990s a draft Convention on International Jurisdiction and Effects of Foreign Judgments in Civil and Commercial Matters was negotiated at The Hague. It was not completed and intellectual property was one of the stumbling blocks.[55] It was eventually decided to remove intellectual property from The Hague process. Since then there have been projects of some depth and breadth to address the complex issues. These include the American Law Institute's detailed framework for a potential international agreement on jurisdiction and choice of law in foreign intellectual property claims,[56] and a European based project prepared by the Max Planck Group.[57] The International Law Association also has a project.[58] Those proposals have not been universally adopted.

The territorial approach often conflicts with the realities of trade in intellectual property both across borders in the traditional sense and in relation to the Internet. Online infringements can occur anywhere and so the choice of one jurisdiction as the place of infringement can seem arbitrary. Territoriality, however, can also have advantages. It provides a way for balancing competing interests and domestic calibration of intellectual property norms to reflect the conditions in each country or region, albeit within a framework of minimum standards. So exceptions appropriate in one country can be enacted and if they are not appropriate in another country they need not be enacted there. This

---

55 See, Hague Conference on Private International Law, "The Judgments Project", www.hcch.net/index_en.php?act=text.display&tid=149, accessed 10 April 2015.

56 F. Dessemontet, R. Dreyfuss and J. Ginsburg, *Intellectual Property Principles Governing Jurisdiction, Choice of Law, and Judgments in Transnational Disputes*, Philadelphia: American Law Institute 2008.

57 European Max Planck Group on Conflict of Laws in Intellectual Property, *Conflict of Laws in Intellectual Property: The Clip Principles and Commentary*, Oxford: Oxford Publishing 2013.

58 International Law Association, Report to the Washington Conference 2014 on *Intellectual Property and Private International Law*, at www.ila-hq.org/en/committees/index.cfm/cid/1037, accessed 22 September 2015.

can produce both desirable and undesirable outcomes. The desirability is that countries have autonomy to utilize intellectual property for local benefit (within the framework of the agreements). The undesirable effects can be for those who rely on exceptions (or rights) in one territory, who may find that what they can do legitimately there they may not be able to do in another market, making cross-border transactions hard or impossible. Short of complete harmonization (which is largely undesirable because of the economic significance of intellectual property and economic differences between countries) this is always, in varying degrees, an effect of minimum standards instruments.

3.2   Principles of treaty interpretation

The public international law customary rules of interpretation of treaties are found in Articles 31 and 32 of the Vienna Convention on the Law of Treaties 1969 (VCLT).[59] The central rule of interpretation and key part of Article 31 of the VCLT requires that: "[a] treaty shall be interpreted in good faith in accordance with the ordinary meaning to be given to the terms of the treaty in their context and in the light of its object and purpose".[60]

The "good faith" requirement is not an abstract requirement, but requires that interpretation should not be used to reach an absurd or unreasonable result. This is important because formalistic or black letter approaches to treaty interpretation, which do not adequately take into account all aspects of ordinary meaning (including the context of terms of a treaty and its object and purpose) can lead to unreasonable results. A treaty interpreter should discern the ordinary

---

59 United Nations, Vienna Convention on the Law of Treaties, 23 May 1969, 1115 U.N.T.S. 331, entered into force 27 January 1980, (hereinafter VCLT), Articles 31–32.

60 VCLT, Article 31 continues to explain context, which is discussed further below. It provides: "2. The context for the purpose of the interpretation of a treaty shall comprise, in addition to the text, including its preamble and annexes: (a) any agreement relating to the treaty which was made between all the parties in connection with the conclusion of the treaty; (b) any instrument which was made by one or more of the parties in connection with the conclusion of the treaty and accepted by the other parties as an instrument related to the treaty. 3. There shall be taken into account, together with the context: (a) any subsequent agreement between the parties regarding the interpretation of the treaty or the application of its provisions; (b) any subsequent practice in the application of the treaty which establishes the agreement of the parties regarding its interpretation; (c) any relevant rules of international law applicable in the relations between the parties. 4. A special meaning shall be given to a term if it is established that the parties so intended."

meaning of an article in a treaty by looking at the words of the article in question and at that article's context and the object and purpose of the treaty.

The primary rule is that the words of the treaty must be interpreted according to their ordinary meaning. The structure of Article 31(1) requires that the context and object and purpose of the treaty are part of the ordinary meaning interpretation exercise. This means that they are tools to locate or discern the ordinary meaning and inform proper interpretation. The effect of this is that treaty interpretation is an exercise that should not be approached as a "black letter" law exercise (or involved an overly formalistic approach) but rather is a much more nuanced and detailed process. This means that while dictionary definitions can be a starting point they are only one factor. An interpreter needs to look at all aspects of Article 31 and may choose to do so in a particular order, but that order should not be mistaken for rigid hierarchical rules. Rather, as the WTO has explained, interpretation in accordance with Article 31 of the VCLT is "holistic":

> The principles of interpretation that are set out in Articles 31 and 32 are to be followed in a holistic fashion. The interpretative exercise is engaged so as to yield an interpretation that is harmonious and coherent and fits comfortably in the treaty as a whole so as to render the treaty provision legally effective. A word or term may have more than one meaning or shade of meaning but the identification of such meaning in isolation only commences the process of interpretation, it does not conclude it. . . . Instead, a treaty interpreter is required to have recourse to context and object and purpose to elucidate the relevant meaning of the word or term. This logical progression provides a framework for proper interpretative analysis. At the same time, it should be kept in mind that treaty interpretation is an integrated operation, where interpretative rules or principles must be understood and applied as connected and mutually reinforcing components of a holistic exercise.[61]

---

61 WTO Appellate Body Report, *United States – Continued Existence and Application of Zeroing Methodology*, WT/DS350/AB/R, (4 February 2009), at [269]. This is an anti-dumping case rather than a dispute under the TRIPS Agreement, but the principles of VCLT interpretation apply equally to all international treaties including WTO agreements. Indeed, the Appellate Body has said that the VCLT rules impose certain common disciplines upon treaty interpreters irrespective of the content of the treaty provision being examined and irrespective of the field of international law concerned (citing WTO Appellate Body Report, *United States – Anti-Dumping Measures on Certain Hot-Rolled Steel Products from Japan*, WT/DS184/AB/R, (24 July 2001), at [60]).

The object and purpose of a treaty can be located in a treaty's pre-amble or sometimes in articles found in the body of the treaty. The VCLT makes it clear that the preamble is part of the context of any treaty. Preambles have on occasion been relied upon by WTO dispute settlement panels.[62] The preamble of the TRIPS Agreement, also includes statements reflecting the object and purpose of the treaty. Articles 7 and 8 of the TRIPS Agreement are also relevant to the object and purpose of TRIPS (see above). The Doha Declaration on the TRIPS Agreement and Public Health expressly states that Articles 7 and 8 are relevant to interpretation of other parts of the TRIPS Agreement.[63] On the face of existing dispute settlement reports, arguably there has not been enough analysis of the object and purpose of the TRIPS Agreement and the purposes of intellectual property more generally.[64]

One of the difficult aspects of treaty interpretation is the timeframe that interpretation should take into account. Is ordinary meaning confined to the time the treaty was made or can it involve assess-ment of what took place after the treaty was concluded? The latter is possible, as a formal matter, if it amounts to a subsequent practice under the VCLT rules. Importantly, subsequent practice is not the practice of one or two parties, rather what can amount to subse-quent practice is practice which "establishes the agreement of parties regarding interpretation" (VCLT, Article 31(3)(b)). More impor-tantly, aspects of intellectual property treaties are designed to be forward looking in order to take into account the dynamic nature of intellectual property. That said a treaty interpreter should not read into a treaty what is not there. In the context of WTO disputes, the DSU expressly provides that dispute settlement should not be used to add to the terms of the treaty or fill any gaps in its coverage. That is the purpose of state-to state negotiation not the role of dispute settlement.[65]

The WIPO Copyright Treaty (WCT) and the WIPO Producers of Phonograms and Sound Recordings Treaty 1996 (WPPT, discussed in

---

62 See WTO Panel Report, *China – Measures Affecting the Protection and Enforcement of Intellectual Property Rights*, WT/DS362/R, (26 January 2009), at [7.501].

63 Doha Declaration, [5.a], WT/MIN (01)/DEC/2, states: "each provision of the TRIPS Agreement shall be read in the light of the object and purpose of the Agreement. . .".

64 S. Frankel, "The WTO's Application of 'the Customary Rules of Interpretation of Public International Law' to Intellectual Property", above note 49.

65 See DSU, Article 19.

sections [4.3.1] and [4.3.2]) include agreed statements.[66] Agreed statements do not necessarily have the same weight as the articles of the treaty but they can be central to interpretation of the treaties key provisions and are aspects of the treaty's context (VCLT, Article 31(2)).

Many terms used in the TRIPS Agreement are specialist intellectual property terms or concepts. In such instances the interpretation process may include looking at norms developed at WIPO, for example, about the meaning and scope of those terms. National laws may also be considered, but as noted above no single national law can be determinative of terms used in an international agreement. Where terms in a treaty are more generalist than intellectual property specialist terms, for example, "public health", then WTO panels or the Appellate Body may look to other international instruments to illuminate the meaning of those terms. The WTO panels and Appellate Body will not look to those other instruments in order to interpret them, rather they will use them in order to shed light on the interpretation of terms in the TRIPS Agreement. This has been done in some non-TRIPS disputes at the WTO.[67]

Also, the VCLT rules provide another avenue through which WTO panels might look at other international instruments. Article 31(3)(c) of the VCLT provides that context includes "any relevant rules of international law applicable in the relations between the parties". There is much commentary and arguably no conclusive determination about whether this rule requires the relevant rules of international law to be "between the parties" to the dispute or "between the parties" to the treaty. The WTO has been cautious about this principle and one panel concluded that "between the parties" must mean all WTO members.[68] The problem with such an interpretation is that when it comes to such a large organization as the WTO no exact replica of parties is likely to be found elsewhere, although the WTO and WIPO have very similar membership. In TRIPS disputes it has not been necessary for

---

66 The WIPO Copyright Treaty, adopted 20 December 1996, WIPO, www.wipo.int/treaties/en/text. jsp?file_id=295166, accessed 26 October 2015 (hereinafter WCT) and the WIPO Performances and Phonograms Treaty, adopted 20 December 1996, www.wipo.int/treaties/en/text.jsp?file_id=295578, accessed 26 October 2015 (hereinafter WPPT).

67 See WTO Appellate Body Report, *United States – Import Prohibition of Certain Shrimp and Shrimp Products*, WT/DS58/AB/R, (12 October 1998).

68 WTO Panel Report, *European Communities – Measures Affecting the Approval and Marketing of Biotech Products*, WT/DS291/R, WT/DS292/R, WT/DS293/R, (29 September 2006) at [7.66]–[7.68].

panels or the Appellate Body to rely on Article 31(3)(c) of the VCLT in order to consider WIPO obligations because of the existing agreement between WIPO and the WTO.

The applicability of Article 31(3)(c) of the VCLT to other international agreements that relate to intellectual property remains unsettled. As a practical matter, however, those other agreements may be referred to as part of the interpretative toolkit relevant to ordinary meaning. The WHO's Framework Convention on Tobacco Control,[69] for example, is arguably a relevant source for interpretation of how "public health" in Article 8 of the TRIPS Agreement applies to the justification of the measures that Australia has taken, which are the subject of a dispute.[70] This use of other international documents to interpret aspects of the TRIPS Agreement (or any international treaty) is important because it links the intellectual property system with other areas of public international law, particularly where those areas may be seen to collide with intellectual property. Importantly, the WTO does not purport to be determinative about other areas of international law, but uses other agreements as interpretative aids. This is because it is not the administrator or "secretariat" of all international law. In addition, treaties outside of the WTO do not necessarily have the same or compatible object and purpose as WTO agreements. Therefore, using them to interpret the TRIPS Agreement (or other WTO agreements) must be done cautiously and so as not to violate the object and purpose of the TRIPS Agreement. As TRIPS incorporates the Berne and Paris Conventions they should also be interpreted consistently.

In the WTO dispute panel report regarding the scope of exceptions under the United States' copyright law, the panel wrote of the need to read the Berne Convention and the TRIPS Agreement as consistently as possible. It then extended that line of reasoning to conclude that the WCT and the TRIPS Agreement should also be read as consistently as possible.

> The WCT is designed to be compatible with this framework, incorporating or using much of the language of the Berne Convention and the TRIPS Agreement. The WCT was unanimously concluded at a diplomatic conference organized under the auspices of WIPO in December

---

69 United Nations Treaty Collection, World Health Organization Framework Convention on Tobacco Control, 21 May 2003, 2302 U.N.T.S. 166, entered into force 27 February 2005.

70 See S. Frankel and D. Gervais, "Plain Packaging and Interpretation of the TRIPS Agreement", 46 *Vanderbilt Journal of Transnational Law* (2013), 1149.

1996 . . . Most of these countries were also participants in the TRIPS negoti-ations and are Members of the WTO. For these reasons, it is relevant to seek contextual guidance also in the WCT when developing interpretations that avoid conflicts within this overall framework, except where these treaties explicitly contain different obligations.[71]

It is questionable whether a treaty subsequent to the TRIPS Agreement that has not been agreed to by all WTO members should provide such interpretative guidance. The approach of the panel was arguably not consistent with the customary international norms of treaty interpre-tation.[72] Yet, there is a kind of expediency in looking at the most recent norms so that a dispute is solved efficaciously.

3.3   Minimum standards, implementing the treaty and more extensive protection

The Conventions which provide for substantive minimum standards (Berne, Paris and the TRIPS Agreement) all require that those mini-mum standards are enacted in domestic law, but leave the mode of implementation to members' discretion. In the TRIPS Agreement this principle is found in Article 1(1), which states that members must comply with the provision of the agreement but that they are "free to determine the appropriate method of implementing the provisions of this Agreement".

In other words, the TRIPS Agreement is not self-executing. This issue is especially important following dispute resolution. If a country is found to be in violation of a provision of TRIPS, that country's legislature must amend its laws before any substantive compliance is put into effect.

One example of the complications that may arise after the implemen-tation of a treaty is the case of *Golan v Holder* in the United States.[73] When the United States implemented the Marrakesh Agreement of 1994 (which included TRIPS), the effect of some provisions of the leg-islation was to take out of the public domain many foreign works that previously had been free to use. The Petitioners in that case argued that

---

71 *US 110(5)*, at [6.70]. This reasoning is questionable, as the WCT was not in force at the time of the Panel decision.

72 See the VCLT.

73 *Golan v Holder*, 609 F. 3d 1076, (10th Cir.) 2010, 132 S.Ct. 873 (2012).

removing works from the public domain violated the United States Constitution. While the Supreme Court held that implementing the international agreement did not violate the Constitution, it is plain to see that once a treaty is ratified at the international level, high hurdles remain between ratification and successful implementation.

The same article of the TRIPS Agreement provides that members may, but shall not be obliged to, provide more extensive protection. The multifaceted nature of this article was confirmed in the panel report of the dispute over enforcement of intellectual property in China, where the WTO panel said:

> The first sentence of Article 1.1 sets out the basic obligation that Members "shall give effect" to the provisions of this Agreement. This means that the provisions of the Agreement are obligations where stated . . . The second sentence of Article 1.1 clarifies that the provisions of the Agreement are minimum standards only, in that it gives Members the freedom to implement a higher standard, subject to a condition. The third sentence of Article 1.1 does not grant Members freedom to implement a lower standard, but rather grants freedom to determine the appropriate method of implementation of the provisions to which they are required to give effect under the first sentence.[74]

The Berne and Paris Conventions also provide that members may provide more extensive protection than the minimum standards required under the agreements in their domestic law. In other words, they can provide more but not less extensive protection. This does not mean that members cannot utilize flexibilities and exceptions provided for in the Agreement. They can, but must do so in compliance with the agreement. There are two broad aspects to this framework that are relevant here. The first is that where the terms used are not prescriptively defined, members may implement those obligations in accordance with their own intellectual property policies. Second, members may provide for exceptions, either under the specific provisions which indicate permissible exceptions or in accordance with the three-step test. Permissible exceptions include, in relation to patents, Articles 27(2) and (3) of the TRIPS Agreement, which respectively permit *ordre public* exceptions and exceptions relating to "diagnostic, therapeutic and surgical methods for the treatment of humans or animals; and plants and animals other than micro-organisms, and essentially

---

74 WTO Panel Report, *China – Measures Affecting the Protection and Enforcement of Intellectual Property Rights*, WT/DS362/R, (20 March 2009), at [7.513].

biological processes for the production of plants or animals other than non-biological and microbiological processes". (The three-step test is discussed in detail in Section [3.6].)

Increases in protection (in other words, more extensive protection) have happened through some multilateral agreements such as the WCT and WPPT discussed below in Sections [4.3.1] and [4.3.2]. Many increases have also occurred through FTAs. FTAs can be bilateral or involve three or more parties, in which case they are plurilateral. We discuss these further in Section [5.6] [issues section, Chapter 5].

The framework of minimum standards is importantly coupled with national treatment and together these important principles form the key framework of the international intellectual property regime.

3.4   National treatment

A legal definition of national treatment is found in Article 3 of the TRIPS Agreement:

> Each Member shall accord to the nationals of other Members treatment no less favourable than that it accords to its own nationals with regard to the protection of intellectual property, subject to the exceptions already provided in, respectively, the Paris Convention (1967), the Berne Convention (1971), the Rome Convention or the Treaty on Intellectual Property in Respect of Integrated Circuits. . .

National treatment simply means that WTO members must treat foreign intellectual property owners at least as well as they treat domestic intellectual property owners. Perhaps perversely, this means that foreigners may be treated better than nationals (for example, by being exempted from certain administrative formalities). International treaties, including the TRIPS Agreement, typically allow members to provide their nationals with greater protection than the standards set down in the treaty.[75] A member that provides greater protection must still apply that protection to foreigners on a national treatment basis.[76]

Suppose country A and country B are both members of the TRIPS Agreement and, in accordance with TRIPS, they provide exclusive

---

75 TRIPS Agreement, Article 1(1).
76 There are some exceptions, see TRIPS Agreement, Article 3(1).

copyright rights to the owners of certain types of copyright works. For convenience we call those exclusive copyright rights: "Apple", "Banana" and "Carrot". Countries A and B both provide these exclusive rights. Country B, in addition, provides exclusive rights to "Eggplant" and "Feijoa". Under the TRIPS Agreement a copyright owner in Country A will receive protection in Country B and will receive protection of all of the exclusive rights in Country B including Eggplant and Feijoa, even though those rights are not available in Country A. This is the effect of national treatment. There are some limited exceptions where reciprocity can apply, rather than national treatment. Significantly, one exception is the term of protection for copyright, which therefore can be applied either on the basis of national treatment or, if TRIPS Agreement and Berne Convention members decide otherwise, on a reciprocal basis.

The opposite of national treatment is material reciprocity – that is "you only get what you give". If material reciprocity applied in the above example, the copyright owner from Country A would only receive the benefits of exclusive rights in Country B that are also available in Country A. In some intellectual property agreements, material reciprocity is substituted for national treatment in relation to specific rights. For example, in the Berne Convention, the requirement to provide an artist's resale right, known as the "*droit de suite*", is subject to reciprocity rather than national treatment. In that situation reciprocity is allowed because the provision of the right is not a compulsory minimum standard that all Berne Convention members must provide: instead it is optional.[77] Also, a country party to the Berne Convention can provide to its nationals a term of protection greater than the standard life plus 50 years, but it need only protect foreign works for the same term that the foreign work receives in its country of origin.[78]

To demonstrate, in the European Union a copyright's standard duration is the life of the author plus 70 years. However, United Kingdom copyright law is drafted so that as of 2015, a Canadian or New Zealand author will only receive the standard Canadian or New Zealand duration: the life of the author plus 50 years.[79] In contrast, although the United States provides the longer 70-year term of protection, it applies

---

77 Berne Convention, Article 14*ter*.

78 Berne Convention, Article 7(8).

79 For discussion of duration see European Council Directive 93/98/EEC, 29 October 1993 replaced in 2006 by Directive 2006/116/EC.

the term on a national treatment basis and does not discriminate against those countries with a shorter term.

The scope of national treatment under the TRIPS Agreement was one of the issues in the *Havana Club* dispute before the WTO in 2001.[80] The dispute concerned United States' laws that prevented legal recognition of any interests of Cuba and Cuban nationals in trademarks and names relating to goods that had been confiscated in Cuba after the Castro revolution. Under these United States' laws, such trademarks could not be registered, renewed, or enforced in the United States without the consent of the original owner. The European Communities (now European Union), the complainant, alleged that the United States' laws in question treated non-United States' nationals less favourably than United States' nationals and were therefore a violation of national treatment. The Appellate Body of the WTO decided that the requirement of consent from original owners was an additional hurdle for foreign nationals and was therefore a national treatment violation.[81]

National treatment in the TRIPS Agreement was also discussed in disputes over the European Union system of registering GIs.[82] Australia and the United States complained that the European Union's system of registration that required foreign countries to have a similar registration system in place, before those foreigners could register GIs in the European Union, violated national treatment. Broadly, the WTO panel found that some, but not all, aspects of the European Union laws violated the national treatment provision. Those that did violate national treatment did so because they embodied different requirements for European Union and non-European Union nationals.

3.5   Most-favoured-nation (MFN) treatment

Article 4 of the TRIPS Agreement provides:

> With regard to the protection of intellectual property, any advantage, favour, privilege or immunity granted by a Member to the nationals of any

---

80 WTO Appellate Body Report, *United States – Section 211 Omnibus Appropriations Act of 1998*, WT/DS176/AB/R, (2 January 2002), (*Havana Club*).

81 *Ibid.*, at [296].

82 WTO Panel Report, *European Communities – Protection of Trademarks and Geographical Indications for Agricultural Products and Foodstuffs*, WT/DS174/R and WT/DS290/R (15 March 2003).

other country shall be accorded immediately and unconditionally to the nationals of all other Members.

The MFN principle – and clause – has its origins in the GATT, the instrument that preceded the Uruguay Round package (which included the Agreement Establishing the WTO and the TRIPS Agreement). The role of MFN in trade negotiations is easy to see. If Country A, a big exporter of good X, is able to secure a reduction in an import tariff or other trade barrier on good X from Country B, then the reduction agreed to by Country B would be extended under MFN to all other GATT parties, including other exporters of X.

The presence of MFN in the TRIPS Agreement is thus essentially a consequence of the TRIPS Agreement being one of the WTO agreements. Under the national treatment clause, intellectual property of foreign origin must be afforded the same rights as intellectual property of domestic origin. MFN treatment, on the other hand, means that any extra benefit provided to a member nation of the WTO, in relation to an intellectual property right, must be provided to all members of the WTO. The MFN clause allows exceptions – that is, favoured treatment of one nation over others – to exist in four key areas:

(a) deriving from international agreements on judicial assistance or law enforcement of a general nature and not particularly confined to the protection of intellectual property;

(b) granted in accordance with the provisions of the Berne Convention (1971) or the Rome Convention authorizing that the treatment accorded be a function not of national treatment but of the treatment accorded in another country;

(c) in respect of the rights of performers, producers of phonograms and broadcasting organizations not provided under this Agreement;

(d) deriving from international agreements related to the protection of intellectual property that entered into force prior to the entry into force of the WTO Agreement, provided that such agreements are notified to the Council for TRIPS and do not constitute an arbitrary or unjustifiable discrimination against nationals of other Members.[83]

Thus, favouritism can also occur in areas that the TRIPS Agreement does not cover. "Favouritism" here means favouring one foreign state over another, rather than a country favouring its own nationals over

---

83 TRIPS Agreement, Article 4.

foreign nationals. In the *Havana Club* dispute – discussed above – the WTO Appellate Body found that the United States' law violated the TRIPS Agreement's MFN article because under the definition of "designated national" in the relevant part of the law, a Cuban was subject to different regulation than a non-Cuban.[84] In other words, non-Cuban's were favoured so Cubans must be equally favoured.

It is important to note that although the MFN clause in the TRIPS Agreement comes from the trade realm, it is different from the MFN clauses in other key WTO agreements and in particular it is different from both GATT and GATS. In GATT and GATS, there is an MFN exemption for the members of a free trade agreement (FTA).[85] In the goods and services context, therefore, the MFN exemption functions (unless members chose otherwise) so that negotiated reduced tariffs and the more liberal market access arising from an FTA are applied only between the members of that agreement and not between other WTO members. The TRIPS Agreement does not have this type of MFN exemption. When members enter into FTAs they may agree to change their domestic laws to a TRIPS-Plus standard – that is, the standards are in addition to the minimum norms required by the TRIPS Agreement. These members will often be required to apply that law on a national treatment basis, unless there is an applicable national treatment exemption.[86] When the domestic law is changed in this way, the MFN principle requires that the law must also be applied to all foreigners in the same way.

3.6 The three-step test[87]

3.6.1 Emergence and dispersion of the three-step test

The first "three-step test" was Article 9(2) of the Berne Convention. It served as a counterweight to the formal recognition of a general right of reproduction in the 1967 Stockholm Act of the Berne Convention.[88] In that version, it reads as follows:

---

84 *Havana Club*, above note 80, at [308]–[309].

85 See GATT, Article XXIV and GATS, Article XIV.

86 TRIPS Agreement, Article 2(1).

87 The authors are grateful to Professors Christophe Geiger and Martin Senftleben for their assistance in preparing the section on the three-step test.

88 It is not entirely accurate to say that the right of reproduction was added to the Berne Convention only at the Stockholm Conference. It was already there in various forms. The Berlin Act of the

It shall be a matter for legislation in the countries of the Union to permit the reproduction of such works in certain special cases, provided that such reproduction does not conflict with a normal exploitation of the work and does not unreasonably prejudice the legitimate interests of the author.

The three "steps" are thus that an exception or limitation to an exclusive right (in this case, copyright, because this version of the test comes from the Berne Convention):

(1) must be a "certain special case";
(2) must not conflict with a normal exploitation of the copyright work; and
(3) must not unreasonably prejudice the legitimate interests of the author.

The interpretation of the test can be informed by its drafting history. As noted above the drafting history is not the first step in interpretation of any treaty provision; according to the Vienna Convention on the Law of Treaties (VCLT), ordinary meaning in context and in light of the object and purpose is the correct approach to interpretation. As a formal VCLT matter, drafting history is only relevant as a supplementary means of interpretation.[89] Drafting history can help to illuminate the object and purpose of a treaty, but it should not be assumed to do so.

The history of the Berne Convention's three-step test includes the following passages in the conference records, in which the steps were considered sequentially:

The Committee also adopted a proposal by the Drafting Committee that the second condition should be placed before the first, as this would afford a more logical order for the interpretation of the rule. If it is considered that reproduction conflicts with the normal exploitation of the work, reproduction is not permitted at all. If it is considered that reproduction

---

Convention (1908) contained several "reproduction rights" or, more precisely perhaps, versions of a more general right of reproduction subsumed under those special mentions. See WIPO, *Berne Convention Centenary*, Geneva: WIPO 1986, at 229. The three-step test was a compromise solution instead of a finite list of specific exceptions, as they are found today in the laws of countries like France, Germany or the Netherlands.

89 VCLT, Article 32 provides: "Recourse may be had to supplementary means of interpretation, including the preparatory work of the treaty and the circumstances of its conclusion, in order to confirm the meaning resulting from the application of article 31, or to determine the meaning when the interpretation according to article 31: (a) leaves the meaning ambiguous or obscure; or (b) leads to a result which is manifestly absurd or unreasonable."

does not conflict with the normal exploitation of the work, the next step would be to consider whether it does not unreasonably prejudice the legitimate interests of the author. Only if such is not the case would it be possible in certain special cases to introduce a compulsory license, or to provide for use without payment.[90]

The test was designed as a guide to national legislators. This *locus* of the test is essential to its interpretation. The notion of "certain special case", if treated as a directive to national legislators, means that a *rule* concerning an exception or limitation must be "special", which one may define as limited-in-scope, or as having a special purpose. Two WTO dispute settlement panels (one relating to a copyright dispute and the other to patents) adopted the limited-in-scope approach.[91] It is arguable that taking the limited-in-scope approach to "certain special cases" is wrong because in the non-copyright three-step tests of the TRIPS Agreement the words "limited exceptions" were used suggesting a different meaning from, and consequently for, the chosen words in the copyright-related three-step test. The qualification of "certain" also arguably suggests a special purpose that is more than just certainty of scope. Whichever of the two approaches of "special cases" is correct the central issue is whether the test is meant to judge the exception *as a rule* rather than its application in a specific case such as to a given author, work and user.

Transposing the wording of the three-step test in national law (that is, changing its status from an international law to a domestic law rule) can radically transform its purpose and meaning. Once transposed into national law, however, as was done, for example, in Australia[92] and in several continental-European countries,[93] the inclusion of the three-step test gives rise to a different question. Depending on the mode of implementation, the test may become a filter for the application of an exception on a case-by-case basis.[94]

---

90 WIPO, "Report on the Work of Main Committee I", in WIPO, *Records of the Intellectual Property Conference of Stockholm June 11 to July 14, 1967*, Geneva: WIPO 1971, at 1145–1146.

91 S. Ricketson and J. C. Ginsburg, *International Copyright and Neighboring Rights: The Berne Convention and Beyond*, above note 36, at 764.

92 Copyright Act 1968 (Australia), Article 200AB and for related purposes, No. 158, 2006, Article 10.

93 The basis for this development is the three-step test in the European Parliament and of the Council, Directive 2001/29/EC, Harmonization of certain rights of copyright and related right in the information society, Article 5(5).

94 For a closer analysis of this development in the European Union, see M.R.F. Senftleben (2009), "Fair Use in the Netherlands – a Renaissance?", *Tijdschrift voor auteurs-, media-en informatierecht* (2009), 33, 1–7, at http://ssrn.com/abstract=1563986; J. Griffiths, "The 'Three-Step Test' in

Since 1967, a version of the test was adopted in four provisions of the TRIPS Agreement (Articles 9, 13, 26(2) and 30). While Articles 9 and 13, like Article 9(2) of the Berne Convention are copyright-related, Article 26(2) deals with designs and Article 30 with patents. In TRIPS the test has thus been extended to almost all areas of intellectual property. It is also used in part (the second step relating to normal exploitation is not expressly included) in Article 17 of the TRIPS Agreement, which deals with trademarks.

In the field of copyright, there is an overlap between two (fairly similar) versions of the test because the test in the Berne Convention (Article 9(2)) was incorporated into TRIPS by Article 9(1) of the TRIPS Agreement. That said, the TRIPS Agreement did not modify the system of exceptions as it exists in the Berne Convention. This means that an exception permitted by another provision of Berne need not be scrutinized under the three-step test as an additional condition.[95] This would be true of provisions such as the exception for reporting of current events (Berne Convention, Article 10(2)), which is subject to its own internal test, namely "to the extent justified by the informatory purpose". Put differently, the TRIPS version of the test applies to new copyright rights added by the TRIPS Agreement[96] and to exceptions not provided specifically in the Berne Convention.

The test has also been incorporated in Articles 10(1) and (2) of the 1996 WCT and Article 16(2) of the WIPO Performances and Phonograms Treaty, both of which are often referred to informally together as the "WIPO Internet Treaties". They are discussed in Sections [4.3.1] and [4.3.2] [Copyright section of Chapter 4].

More recently, the test appears in Article 13(2) of the 2012 Beijing Treaty on Audio-visual Performances and Article 11 of the 2013 Marrakesh Treaty to Facilitate Access to Published Works for Persons who are

---

European Copyright Law – Problems and Solutions", *Intellectual Property Quarterly*, (2009), 489, at 495; C. Geiger, "The Three-Step Test, A Threat to a Balanced Copyright Law?", 37 *International Review of Intellectual Property and Competition Law* (2006), 683–699; C. Geiger, "From Berne to National Law, via the Copyright Directive: The Dangerous Mutations of the Three-Step Test", *European Intellectual Property Review* (2007), 486.

95 For example, exception and limitations for compulsory licensing in the field of cable distribution, Berne Convention, Article 11*bis*(2) and sound recordings, Berne Convention, Article 13(1), are self-contained.

96 For example, the rental right in TRIPS Agreement, Articles 11 and 14(4).

Blind, Visually Impaired or Otherwise Print Disabled, which are also presented briefly in Section [4.3.4] [Copyright section of Chapter 4].

Table 3.1 shows the variations on the three-step test.

This evolution in the role and scope of the test and the related changes in the language, sometimes quite significantly, is a notable concern and poses interpretation difficulties. For example, in Articles 26(2) and 30 of the TRIPS Agreement, "special" was replaced by "limited". In Article 13 of the TRIPS Agreement, "author" was replaced by "right holder" (as if media and communications companies exploiting works of authors always had coextensive interests with those of authors[97]). In two instantiations of the test in the TRIPS Agreement (Articles 26(2) and 30), the legitimate interests *of third parties* were added to the third step, a significant change to be sure. As noted in a WTO dispute settlement panel report dealing with the three-step test, this seems to change the normative equation of the third step because users' interests may not be of the same nature as those of "right holders".[98] It also begs the question what happens in copyright (Article 13 of the TRIPS Agreement and Article 9(2) of the Berne Convention, as incorporated into TRIPS) where interests of third parties (such as those of users) are not mentioned. In copyright the purpose of limitation and exceptions sometimes states a kind of third-party interest such as for research or parody. This points towards such purposes being relevant to the three-step test and particularly the first step and the approach

---

97 The notion of "author" in the Berne Convention seems to presuppose that the author is a living crea-tor. For example the default term of protection of copyright in the Convention is the life of the author plus 50 years, Berne Convention, Article 7. Still, in the case of collective works (for example, an ency-clopaedia), a number of countries recognize that a legal person (corporation or other such entity) can be the author, as can be the case in the United States under the "work made for hire" doctrine.

98 For an overview of related WTO Dispute Settlement cases, see D. Gervais, *The TRIPS Agreement: Drafting History and Analysis*, 4th ed., London: Sweet & Maxwell, 2012, at 282–292 and at 474–475; C. M. Correa, *Trade-Related Aspects of Intellectual Property Rights: A Commentary on the TRIPS Agreement*, Oxford: Oxford University Press, 2007; M.R.F. Senftleben, "Towards a Horizontal Standard for Limiting Intellectual Property Rights? – WTO Panel Reports Shed Light on the Three-Step Test in Copyright Law and Related Tests in Patent and Trademark Law", 37(4) *International Review of Intellectual Property and Competition Law* (2006), 407; M. Ficsor, "How Much of What? The Three-Step Test and Its Application in Two Recent WTO Dispute Settlement Cases", *Revue International du Droit d'Auteur* (2002), 192, 111; D. J. Brennan, "The Three-Step Test Frenzy: Why the TRIPS Panel Decision might be considered Per Incuriam", *Intellectual Property Quarterly* (2002), 213; J. C. Ginsburg, "Toward Supranational Copyright Law? The WTO Panel Decision and the "Three-Step Test" for Copyright Exceptions", *Revue International du Droit d'Auteur* (2001), 13; C. Geiger, "The Role of the Three-Step Test in the Adaptation of Copyright Law to the Information Society", *e-Copyright Bulletin* January–March 2007.

Table 3.1 The three-step test: similarities and differences

TREATY	ARTICLE TEXT	POINTS TO NOTE (more detail is found in the discussion)
Berne Convention for the Protection of Literary and Artistic Works (Berne Convention)	Article 9(2) It shall be a matter for legislation in the countries of the Union to permit the reproduction of such works in certain special cases, provided that such reproduction does not conflict with a normal exploitation of the work and does not unreasonably prejudice the legitimate interests of the author.	*The steps are:* *1. must be a "certain special case";* *2. must not conflict with a normal exploitation of the copyright work; and* *3. must not unreasonably prejudice the legitimate interests of the author.* *This test is the first instance of the three-step test. It is for exceptions to the right of reproduction in copyright.*
Agreement on Trade-Related Aspects of Intellectual Property Rights (1996)	Article 9(1) (1) Members shall comply with Articles 1 through 21 of the Berne Convention (1971) and the Appendix thereto. However, Members shall not have rights or obligations under this Agreement in respect of the rights conferred under Article 6*bis* of that Convention or of the rights derived therefrom.	*This Article provides that the three-step test, as found in the Berne Convention Article 9(2), is incorporated into the TRIPS Agreement. It is not, however, the only three-step test in TRIPS (see below).*

Table 3.1 (continued)

TREATY	ARTICLE TEXT	POINTS TO NOTE (more detail is found in the discussion)
(TRIPS Agreement)	Article 13 Members shall confine limitations or exceptions to exclusive rights to certain special cases which do not conflict with a normal exploitation of the work and do not unreasonably prejudice the legitimate interests of the right holder.	*The steps in this case are:* *1. must be a "certain special case";* *2. must not conflict with a normal exploitation of the work;* *3. must not unreasonably prejudice the legitimate interests of the right holder.* *This three-step test is applicable to copyright. The two main differences between Article 13 TRIPS and Article 9(2) of the Berne Convention are first, the extension of the test to exceptions to rights other than reproduction and second, that "author" is exchanged for "right holder" in step three.*
	Article 17 Members may provide limited exceptions to the rights conferred by a trademark, such as fair use of descriptive terms, provided that such exceptions take account of the legitimate interests of the owner of the trademark and of third parties.	*The steps in this case are two rather than three; there is no reference to the normal exploitation of the work (step two):* *Unlike Article 13 this Article (and like Article 30) refers in the third step to the interest of third parties.* *This version of the three-step test is the only one that gives an example; "fair use of descriptive terms".*

Article 26(2)

Members may provide limited exceptions to the protection of industrial designs, provided that such exceptions do not unreasonably conflict with the normal exploitation of protected industrial designs and do not unreasonably prejudice the legitimate interests of the owner of the protected design, taking account of the legitimate interests of third parties.

Article 30

Members may provide limited exceptions to the exclusive rights conferred by a patent, provided that such exceptions do not unreasonably conflict with a normal exploitation of the patent and do not unreasonably prejudice the legitimate interests of the patent owner, taking account of the legitimate interests of third parties.

The steps in this case are:
1. *there must be a limited exception;*
2. *must not unreasonably conflict with the normal exploitation of protected industrial designs;*
3. *must not unreasonably prejudice the legitimate interests of the owner of the protected designer, taking account of the legitimate interests of third parties.*

Like Articles 17 and 30 the third step includes not only the legitimate interests of the owner but also of third parties.

"Unreasonably" is added to step two, unlike Article 13.

The steps in this case are:
1. *there must be a limited exception;*
2. *must not unreasonably conflict with a normal exploitation of the patent;*
3. *must not unreasonably prejudice the legitimate interests of the patent owner, taking into account the legitimate interests of third parties.*

This test also includes "unreasonably" in step two (Article 13 does not) and includes legitimate third party interests in addition to the owner's interest in the third step.

Table 3.1 (continued)

TREATY	ARTICLE TEXT	POINTS TO NOTE (more detail is found in the discussion)
WIPO Copyright Treaty (1996) (WCT)	Article 10 (1) Contracting Parties may, in their national legislation, provide for limitations of or exceptions to the rights granted to authors of literary and artistic works under this Treaty in certain special cases that do not conflict with a normal exploitation of the work and do not unreasonably prejudice the legitimate interests of the author. (2) Contracting Parties shall, when applying the Berne Convention, confine any limitations of or exceptions to rights provided for therein to certain special cases that do not conflict with a normal exploitation of the work and do not unreasonably prejudice the legitimate interests of the author.	*This Article does not vary the Berne test and adopts the similar wording to Article 9(2) of the Berne Convention.* *The aim is to apply the test in the digital world.*
WIPO Performances and Phonograms Treaty (1996) (WPPT)	Article 16(2) Contracting Parties shall confine any limitations of or exceptions to rights provided for in this Treaty to certain special cases which do not conflict with a normal exploitation of the performance or phonogram and do not unreasonably prejudice the legitimate interests of the performer or of the producer of the phonogram.	*By reiterating the wording of Article 9(2) of the Berne Convention, this Article extends the test to apply in circumstances relating to performances and phonograms and the associated rights that the WPPT is about.* *The aim is to apply the test in the digital world.*

Beijing Treaty on Audio-visual Performances (2012)	Article 13(2) Contracting Parties shall confine any limitations of or exceptions to rights provided for in this Treaty to certain special cases which do not conflict with a normal exploitation of the performance and do not unreasonably prejudice the legitimate interests of the performer.	*Following on from the WPPT, this extended the use of the three-step test to audio-visual performances, which were not necessarily covered in the WPPT. This is another example of the test being employed in treaties to ensure those same limitations and exceptions are applied as technology advances.*
Marrakesh Treaty to Facilitate Access to Published Works for Persons who are Blind, Visually Impaired or Otherwise Print Disabled (2013)	Article 11 In adopting measures necessary to ensure the application of this Treaty, a Contracting Party may exercise the rights and shall comply with the obligations that that Contracting Party has under the Berne Convention, the Agreement on Trade-Related Aspects of Intellectual Property Rights and the WIPO Copyright Treaty, including their interpretative agreements so that: (a) in accordance with Article 9(2) of the Berne Convention, a Contracting Party may permit the reproduction of works in certain special cases provided that such reproduction does not conflict with a normal exploitation of the work and does not unreasonably prejudice the legitimate interests of the author;	*This Article includes the three-step test as articulated in other copyright related treaties described above.*

Table 3.1 (continued)

TREATY	ARTICLE TEXT	POINTS TO NOTE (more detail is found in the discussion)
	(b) in accordance with Article 13 of the Agreement on Trade-Related Aspects of Intellectual Property Rights, a Contracting Party shall confine limitations or exceptions to exclusive rights to certain special cases which do not conflict with a normal exploitation of the work and do not unreasonably prejudice the legitimate interests of the rightholder;	
	(c) in accordance with Article 10(1) of the WIPO Copyright Treaty, a Contracting Party may provide for limitations of or exceptions to the rights granted to authors under the WCT in certain special cases, that do not conflict with a normal exploitation of the work and do not unreasonably prejudice the legitimate interests of the author;	
	(d) in accordance with Article 10(2) of the WIPO Copyright Treaty, a Contracting Party shall confine, when applying the Berne Convention, any limitations of or exceptions to rights to certain special cases that do not conflict with a normal exploitation of the work and do not unreasonably prejudice the legitimate interests of the author.	

that it must be a "certain special case". Although, as noted above, the WTO cases have applied "limited-in-scope" rather than "special". The purpose of the exception seems most suited to being part of the analysis under the first step, in view of the panel's approach it should therefore arguably be taken into account in the second step, in other words, what amounts to normal exploitation. One thing is for sure, the purpose of the exception should be included in the analysis of the test.

In addition, the TRIPS test is not limited to the reproduction right. At least as far as the new copyright subject matter and rights in the TRIPS Agreement are concerned there can thus be exceptions to exclusive rights other than reproduction. The Berne Convention contains other exceptions and limitations (for example, the possibility of issuing compulsory licenses for broadcasting Article 11*bis*(1) and making sound recordings of a published musical work (Article 13(1)). Those should not be subject to the TRIPS Agreement three-step test in addition to complying with the Berne Convention requirements. The same may be said of other Berne Convention exceptions, such as quotation (Article 10(1), which is framed in mandatory terms: "[i]t shall be permissible to make quotations from a work which has already been lawfully made available to the public...."). However, as confirmed by the panel in the *US 110(5)* dispute, when an exception that has historically been accepted by Berne Union members is not subject to clear constraints in the Berne Convention, then the TRIPS three-step test may be used to set appropriate limits.[99]

The function of the three-step test as a flexible framework for the adoption of exceptions and limitations at the national level emerges quite clearly in the 1996 "WIPO Internet treaties",[100] and specifically in the agreed statement concerning WCT, Article 10:

> It is understood that the provisions of Article 10 permit Contracting Parties to carry forward and appropriately extend into the digital environment limitations and exceptions in their national laws which have been considered acceptable under the Berne Convention. Similarly, these provisions should be understood to permit Contracting Parties to devise new exceptions and limitations that are appropriate in the digital network environment. It is also understood that Article 10(2) neither reduces nor extends the scope

---

99 *US – 110(5)*, above note 24, [6.80]–[6.82].
100 WCT and WPPT.

of applicability of the limitations and exceptions permitted by the Berne Convention.

The agreed statement concerning Article 10 confirms the desirability of maintaining an appropriate balance in copyright law. The Statement maintains the legality of Berne-compatible exceptions and limitations without changing the role of the test in that context (Article 10 allows Contracting Parties "to carry forward and appropriately extend into the digital environment limitations and exceptions in their national laws *which have been considered acceptable under the* Berne Convention" (emphasis added)).

Interestingly, the Marrakesh Treaty to Facilitate Access to Published Works for Persons Who Are Blind, Visually Impaired, or Otherwise Print Disabled, signed on 27 June 2013, explicitly refers to different versions of the "three-step test" in international copyright law. Article 11 of the Treaty makes it clear that there are many versions of the test and that an exception or limitation must comply with all versions which a country is bound by under the Berne Convention, the TRIPS Agreement and the WCT, including their interpretative agreements. This arguably supports interpretations of the test(s) in TRIPS, for example, that differ from earlier interpretations under the Berne Convention. This is so even though it is to be taken into account that the WCT, according to its Article 1(1), is a special agreement within the meaning of Article 20 of the Berne Convention, and that WTO panels may rely on the Berne *acquis* when it comes to the interpretation of the three-step test in Article 13 of the TRIPS Agreement.[101]

3.6.2   Interpretation of the three-step test

Three WTO dispute settlement panels have interpreted the test thus far. On 15 June 2000,[102] a WTO dispute settlement panel found that the United States had adopted a copyright exception in violation of Article 13 of the TRIPS Agreement. The WTO panel stated that section 110(5) (b) of the United States Copyright Act, which exonerates certain com-

---

101   This approach has been taken by the WTO Panel dealing with section 110(5) of the US Copyright Act. In the WTO Report of the Panel, above note 24, [6.62], the Panel explicitly held that the inclusion of Berne provisions by virtue of TRIPS Agreement Article 9(1) included the Berne *acquis*: "If that incorporation should have covered only the text of Articles 1–21 of the Berne Convention (1971), but not the entire Berne *acquis* relating to these articles, Article 9.1 of the TRIPS Agreement would have explicitly so provided."

102   *US – 110(5)*, above note 24.

mercial establishments such as bars or restaurants that broadcast non-dramatic musical works from copyright royalty payments,[103] violated *all three steps* of Article 13 of the TRIPS Agreement.[104] For the first time, an international dispute settlement panel also offered a formal and detailed definition of the conditions set by the test in the field of copyright law.

This dispute underscored that the three-step test had to be taken seriously and that further work was required on understanding the flexibilities and limits on national legislators' freedom to implement copyright exceptions and limitations. Because of the panel's interpretation (and the enforceability of WTO dispute settlement panel reports), the three-step test has become one of the main, if not *the main* issue, when trying to calibrate domestic law to find a fair balance of interests in copyright law and policy. Because of its expansion to most areas of intellectual property, the test is the focal point for almost all exceptions and limitations to intellectual property rights. We now turn to consider the WTO disputes that interpreted the three-step tests.

The United States – *Section 110(5) dispute*

The European Union (then the European Communities) brought this dispute to the WTO. It alleged that what are known as the business exemption and the homestyle exemption, of section 110(5) of the United States Copyright Act, were not compliant with the three-step test. The details of the United States' provision are lengthy as was the evidence put to the WTO panel. In sum, the homestyle exception allowed for the use of homestyle equipment to play copyright musical works in retail establishments of a certain size. The business exception allowed other sorts of equipment and playing of the copyright works in larger establishments. Much of the panel's analysis of the three-step test focused on the commerciality of the business exemption and the more "limited" nature of the homestyle exemption.

According to the WTO dispute settlement panel, the first condition of the test (namely the requirement of a "certain special case" or that an exception be "limited" in other versions of the test), implied that "an exception or limitation in national legislation must be clearly defined" (which corresponds to the requirement of a "certain" case) and that it has "an individual or limited application or purpose" (which corresponds

---

103   17 U.S.C. § 100 (5), as modified by an act of 1998 (Fairness in Music Licensing Act).
104   Concerning this decision, see for example, M.R.F. Senftleben, above note 98, at 407–438.

to the requirement of a "special" case). The WTO panel drew a significant distinction between the words "certain" and "special". It interpreted the term "certain" to mean that an exception and limitation had to be clearly defined, though there was no need "to identify explicitly each and every possible situation to which the exception could apply, provided that the scope of the exception was known and particularised".[105] The panel thus regarded the word "certain" as a guarantee of a sufficient degree of legal certainty.[106]

From the term "special", the panel derived the additional requirement that an exception should be *narrow in a quantitative as well as a qualitative sense*.[107] It summarized this twofold requirement as narrowness in "scope and reach".[108] Its application to the business exemption and the homestyle exemption of section 110(5) shows that, pursuant to the panel's conception, it is particularly the number of potential beneficiaries that must be sufficiently limited in order to comply with the quantitative aspect of "special".[109] As to the qualitative aspect, the panel eschewed an inquiry into the legitimacy of the public policy purpose underlying the adoption of the exception at hand.[110] In the panel's view, the qualitative aspect of "special" did not mean that an exception or limitation must necessarily serve a special purpose to be qualified as a special case under Article 13 of the TRIPS Agreement.[111] Unfortunately the panel also did not say that a special purpose could also amount to a special case. Instead, the panel raised conceptual qualitative issues, such as the categories of works affected by an exception or limitation and the circumstances under which it may be invoked.

The second step has the potential to restrict considerably the freedom of national legislation to enact new exceptions and limitations. That step is the prohibition of a conflict with a "normal exploitation" of the work. How is the phrase "normal exploitation" to be interpreted? In the panel's report in the *US – 110(5)* case, the criterion of normal exploi-

---

105   *US – 110(5)*, above note 24, at para. 6.108.
106   The Panel held, for instance, that the term "homestyle equipment" was sufficiently clear and that detailed technical specifications were not necessary. *Ibid*, [6.145].
107   See, *ibid.*, [6.109].
108   See *ibid.*, [6.112].
109   See *ibid.*, [6.127] and [6.143].
110   See *ibid.*, [6.111].
111   See *ibid.*, [6.112]. Cf. J. C. Ginsburg, "Toward Supranational Copyright Law? The WTO Panel Decision and the 'Three-Step Test' for Copyright Exceptions", above note 98; S. Ricketson, "The three-step test, deemed quantities, libraries and closed exceptions", Strawberry Hills NSW: Centre for Copyright Studies, (2002), 31.

tation was deemed to involve consideration of the forms of exploitation that *currently generate income* for the right holder as well as those
which, in all probability, *are likely to be of considerable importance
in the future.*[112] In other words, it included an empirical approach to
normal based on fact and a normative approach based on the suite of
exclusive rights, whether copyright owners in the relevant fields "normally" exploit the rights or not. This might suggest that making fair
use of or fair dealing with a copyright work and creating a new market,
which has not been previously exploited by a copyright owner (in some
jurisdictions as a type of transformative use) could arguably fail the
three-step test. Of course each decision at national law will turn on its
facts, but it is problematic to read the three-step test very narrowly if
such a reading creates lack of equilibrium between rights and limitations and exceptions. The three-step test should be extended to new
technologies just as the rights can be interpreted to do so.

Under the third step, an exception must be prevented from causing an
unreasonable prejudice to the legitimate interests of the right holder.
This language indicates that the right holder is not intended to have
the power to control *all* uses of a protected work. Indeed, it suggests
that some interests may not be "legitimate" in this context, and that a
certain amount of prejudice is acceptable.[113]

Given those safeguards, the formulation of the third step allows
WTO members to use a *proportionality* test.[114] A legislature or judge
applying the third step of the test can therefore consider the policy
justification(s) behind the exception.

The Canada – Pharmaceuticals *dispute*

In the *Canada – Pharmaceuticals* dispute,[115] a different WTO panel
seemed to adhere to a more normative approach in interpreting

---

112 *US – 110(5)*, above note 24, [6.180].

113 In this sense also, *ibid.*, [6.222] and [6.229], noting that "a certain amount of 'prejudice' has to be
    presumed justified as 'not unreasonable'".

114 M. R. F. Senftleben, *Copyright, Limitations and the Three-Step Test: An Analysis of the Three-
    Step Test in International and EC Copyright Law*, (Kluwer Law International, 2004), at 226;
    S. Dusollier, *Droit d'auteur et protection des œuvres dans l'univers numérique*, (Larcier 2005),
    at 221. See also C. Geiger, "The Three-Step Test, A Threat to a Balanced Copyright Law?", 37
    International Review of Intellectual Property and Competition Law (2006), 683, at 696.

115 WTO Panel Report, *Canada – Patent Protection of Pharmaceutical Products*, WT/DS114/R,
    (17 March 2000), (*Canada Pharmaceuticals*).

Article 30 of the TRIPS Agreement – the three-step test version applicable to exceptions to patent rights.[116] According to the report, "exploitation" should be considered "normal" when it is "essential to the
achievement of the goals of patent policy".[117] That formulation remains
somewhat vague, but it seems to provide the possibility for legislatures to take normative elements into account instead of confining the
analysis to a strictly economic approach.[118] Admittedly, the wording
of the second step (in the version contained in Article 30) is different
from the parallel criterion in the copyright provision in Article 13 of
the TRIPS Agreement. Under Article 30, "exceptions must not *unreasonably* conflict with a normal exploitation of the patent" (emphasis
added). Similarly, according to Article 26(2) of the TRIPS Agreement,
which applies to design rights, "members may provide limited exceptions to the protection of industrial designs, provided that such exceptions do not *unreasonably* conflict with the normal exploitation of
protected industrial designs" (emphasis added). The explicit reference
to a notion such as the "reasonableness" of the restriction to the exclusive right allows taking into account other interests than those of the
right holder.[119] Article 30 and Article 26(2) of the TRIPS Agreement
thus allow a more broader and likely therefore more flexible application of the test than in Article 13 of the TRIPS Agreement or Article
9(2) of the Berne Convention.[120] However, there is no stated reason
in TRIPS to explain why restrictions to the rights of the owner of a
patent or of an industrial design should be treated differently from
those of the owner of authors' rights/copyright. In addition, the patent
test in the third step refers to third-party interests. The panel did not
discuss in any great detail what this means, but in the patent context
it may mean, for example, consumers (including would-be consumers)

---

116 TRIPS Agreement, Article 30: "Members may provide limited exceptions to the exclusive rights
conferred by a patent, provided that such exceptions do not unreasonably conflict with a normal
exploitation of the patent and do not unreasonably prejudice the legitimate interests of the
patent owner, taking account of the legitimate interests of third parties."

117 *Canada Pharmaceuticals*, above note 115, at [7.58]. On this report, see. M. R. F. Senftleben,
above note 98.

118 More generally, for an analysis of exclusions to Patent Law provisions in TRIPS from an international Human Rights perspective, see H. M. Haugen, "Human Rights and TRIPS Exclusion and
Exception Provisions", 11(5/6) *Journal of World Intellectual Property*, (2009), 345–374.

119 See Chapter 1.

120 As A. Kur, "Of Oceans, Islands, and Inland Water – How much Room for Exceptions and
Limitations under the Three-step Test?", 8(3) *Richmond Journal of Global Law and Business*
(2009), 288, at 287, points out, the drafting history of the TRIPS Agreement also does not offer
an explanation as to why these differences in wording occurred and whether they were intended
to have a special meaning.

of patented products such as pharmaceuticals. What is clear, however, from the panel report is that the interests in question are not limited to legal interests,[121] and include "a normative claim calling for protection of interests that are "justifiable" in the sense that they are supported by relevant public policies or other social norms".[122]

The legitimate interests of the patent owner mean more than just the *de jure* interests that are included in the patent exclusive rights part of the TRIPS Agreement. In the dispute, the question was whether the *de facto* extension of a patent term, which arose from potential competitors being unable to launch their product on the market the day that the patent expired because of regulatory requirements, was a legitimate interest of the patentee.[123] The panel held it was not a legitimate interest of the patentee that flowed from its patent rights. Importantly, although the "interest" at issue was more than "legal", it flowed not from the articulated patent legal rights but as a consequence of the requirements of a regulatory regime outside of patent law. Put differently, the panel's reference to rights other than the legal ones cannot reasonably extend to everything. It includes *de facto* interests that flow from the patent legal rights or are connected in some way to the patent legal rights. The panel's reasoning was that confining the meaning of legitimate interests to legal rights would make the reference to legitimate interests of third parties redundant, as third parties had no patent legal rights. The panel said that "reading the third condition as a further protection of legal rights would render it essentially redundant in light of the very similar protection of legal rights in the first condition of Article 30 ('limited exception')".[124]

In view of this approach to the third step it becomes questionable why the second step, normal exploitation, must include both a normative and empirical analysis. It might make more sense for one step to tackle the normative and the other the empirical.

The EU – geographical indications *dispute*

Although Article 17 of the TRIPS Agreement (the exceptions framework for trademarks) does not include all three steps of the test it is

---

121 *Canada Pharmaceuticals*, above note 115, at [7.73].

122 *Ibid.* at [7.69].

123 *Ibid.*, at [2.1]–[2.7].

124 *Ibid.*, at [7.68].

useful to discuss, both because its test is derivative of the three-step test and because of the panel's insights into the third step. The insights may be primarily relevant to trademark law. However, there are many areas of trademark law relating to expressive issues that overlap with copyright. Thus, treating the tests as not having any overlap and too separate from each other may well be flawed. The panel report in the *EC-Geographical Indications* dispute pointed out the similarities and differences between Article 17 and other instantiations of the three-step test under Articles 13, 26(2), and 30 of the TRIPS Agreement, as well as Article 9(2) of the Berne Convention, as incorporated by Article 9(1) of the TRIPS Agreement.[125] Unlike these other provisions, Article 17 contains no reference to "conflict with a normal exploitation", no reference to "unreasonable prejudice" to the legitimate interests of the right holder or owner, and it not only refers to the legitimate interests of third parties but also treats them on par with those of the right holder.[126] It is also the only one of these provisions that contains an example (namely, fair use of descriptive terms). The panel concluded that the European Union exception at issue was limited within the meaning of this article but cautioned that "[i]f the [GI] registration prevented the trademark owner from exercising its rights against these signs, combinations of signs, or linguistic versions, which do not appear expressly in the GI registration, it would seriously expand the exception and undermine the limitations on its scope".[127] It found that the legitimate interests of the trademark owner must be something different than full enjoyment of legal rights and that the legitimate interests of third parties were something different from simply the enjoyment of their legal rights. The panel said:

> every trademark owner has a legitimate interest in preserving the distinctiveness, or capacity to distinguish, of its trademark so that it can perform that function. This includes its interest in using its own trademark in connection with the relevant goods and services of its own and authorized undertakings. Taking account of that legitimate interest will also take account of the trademark owner's interest in the economic value of its mark arising from the reputation that it enjoys and the quality that it denotes.[128]

---

125 WTO Panel Report, *European Communities – Protection of Trademarks and Geographical Indications for Agricultural Products and Foodstuffs, Complaint by the United States* WT/DS174/R, (15 March 2005), at [7.649].
126 *Ibid.*
127 *Ibid.*, at [7.657].
128 *Ibid.*, at [7.664].

The panel concluded that the European Union regulation did "take account" of those legitimate interests, adding that "the proviso to Article 17 requires only that exceptions 'take account' of the legitimate interests of the owner of the trademark, and does not refer to 'unreasonabl[e] prejudice' to those interests", which "suggests that a lesser standard of regard for the legitimate interests of the owner of the trademark is required".[129]

Alternative approaches to interpreting the three-step test

Alternative approaches in interpreting the test have been suggested. One alternative approach is for greater account to be taken in dispute settlement of the normative purpose of any exception at domestic law. An example of this is, as noted above, recognition of the policy purpose more fully as part of the interpretation of the first step in the copyright test, "certain special case". Another suggested approach is that a more normative application of the three-step test might be mandated by international obligations resulting from treaties protecting human rights and fundamental rights.[130] International obligations can result, for example, from the Universal Declaration of Human Rights (UDHR) of 1948 and the International Covenant on Economic, Social and Cultural Rights (ICESCR) of 19 December 1966. Both may be seen as providing guidelines for the interpretation of the TRIPS Agreement, and therefore also of the three-step test. Such an interpretation of TRIPS in the light of international fundamental rights provisions could result from the general rule of interpretation of treaties to be found in Article 31 of the VCLT.[131] There are two relevant approaches. The first is that the human rights obligations are part of the interpretation of the three-step test in light of the object and purpose of the TRIPS

---

129 *Ibid.*, at [7.671].

130 C. Geiger, "Exploring the Flexibilities of the TRIPS Agreement Provisions on Limitations and Exceptions" in: A. Kur and V. Mizaras (eds.), *The Structure of Intellectual Property Law – Can One Size Fit All?*, (Edward Elgar 2011), 287, at 297.

131 See VCLT, Articles 31 and 32, which relate explicitly to interpretation (other parts of the VCLT are about other rules of international law) and are explicitly included in the WTO's Dispute Settlement Understanding, Article 3(2), which refers to the customary rules of interpretation of public international law. Successive panels and the Appellate Body recognize the role of Articles 31 and 32 of the VCLT in interpretation of the WTO agreements and it is beyond dispute that they are the key "procedural code" in this sphere. However, it is true that some important WTO members such as the United States have not ratified the whole of the VCLT. If the VCLT is customary international law that may be irrelevant. It is in any event irrelevant with regard to the rules of interpretation in Articles 31 and 32. Also in many WTO disputes other parts of the VCLT have been relied on by panels and the Appellate Body.

Agreement, including Articles 7 and 8 (see the discussion in Section [3.2] [interpretation section of book]). The other approach is that under Article 31(3)(c) of the VCLT, for the interpretation of a treaty "any relevant rules of international law applicable in the relations between the parties" should be taken into account.[132] Given the ethical questions involved, it is hard to completely exclude the relevance of the UDHR.

Those who support a reading of the three-step test that departs from the *US – 110(5)* panel report point to the fact that a number of national courts have interpreted the test in a more liberal manner than the WTO panel.[133]

Another approach would be to read the test as simply stating factors that need to be considered, based on the model of the American fair use doctrine according to which a use can be deemed fair after the analysis of four factors.[134] Those who support this approach draw a parallel with the fourth factor contained in Article 107 of the United States Copyright Act, which codified the doctrine elaborated by United States' courts since the nineteenth century. According to this fourth factor, the *effect of the use on the potential market* for or value of the copyrighted work must be taken into account in determining whether a particular use is fair. Similarly, one could say that the second step (impact on normal exploitation of the work) is *one of the criteria* to take into account during the analysis of the application of an exception or exceptions and limitations, but not the only one. Under this type of approach, the three-step test could be renamed the "three-factor test".

---

132 For a discussion of the full role of Article 31(3)(c) see S. Frankel, "WTO Application of 'the Customary Rules of Interpretation of Public International Law' to Intellectual Property", above note 49, 365, at 420.

133 See for example the decision of the Swiss Supreme Court, 1st Civil Division, 26 June 2007, *International Review of Intellectual Property and Competition Law* 39 (2008), p. 990. For a comment see C. Geiger, "Rethinking Copyright Limitations in the Information Society: The Swiss Supreme Court Leads the Way", 39 *International Review of Intellectual Property and Competition Law* (2008), 943; Court of Appeal of Barcelona (SAP), 17 September 2008.

134 K. J. Koelman, "Fixing the Three-step Test", *European Intellectual Property Review*, (2006), 407; M. R. F. Senftleben, "L'application du triple test: vers un système de fair use européen", *Propr. Intell.* (2007), 453; and from the same author: "Fair Use in the Netherlands – A Renaissance?", *Tijdschrift voor auteurs-, media-en informatierecht* (2009), 1, at 7: "The adoption of a fair use system that rests on the flexible, open criteria of a conflict with a normal exploitation and an unreasonable prejudice to the legitimate interests would pave the way for this more flexible and balanced application of the test."

Finally, the Declaration on a Balanced Interpretation of the Three-Step Test, prepared by a group of scholars from several different jurisdictions, is also worth mentioning. It considered the test as an indivisible entirety requiring a comprehensive overall assessment.[135]

---

135 See C. Geiger, J. Griffiths and R. M. Hilty, "Declaration on a Balanced Interpretation of the "Three-Step Test" in Copyright Law", 39 *Int'l Review Intellectual Property and Competition Law* (2008), 707. The aim of this declaration was "to restore the 'three-step test' to its original role as a relatively flexible standard precluding clearly unreasonable encroachments upon an author's rights without interfering unduly with the ability of legislatures and courts to respond to the challenges presented by shifting commercial and technological contexts in a fair and balanced manner", C. Geiger, J. Griffiths and R. M. Hilty, "Towards a Balanced Interpretation of the 'Three-step test' in Copyright Law", *European Intellectual Property Review* (2008), 489. See also. R. M. Hilty, "Declaration on the Three-Step Test – Where do we go from here?", 1 *Journal Intellectual Property, Information Technology and E-Commerce Law* (2010), 83.

4 The current norms of international intellectual property

In previous chapters, we covered a number of key concepts and norms of international intellectual property. We also saw how disputes are settled, and the role and history of WIPO and the WTO. The previous chapter also presented a summary of the types of norms contained in each major instrument. In this chapter we consider each specific area of intellectual property as a network across agreements and institutions. The multiplicity of institutions and agreements, as the above chapters suggest, means that international intellectual property is complicated. The more institutions that become involved as the effects of globalized intellectual property rights are felt, the more complex the regime arguably becomes. With that complexity comes a diverse range of views and approaches which ultimately can serve to enrich the discourse and understanding of the role and function of intellectual property law.

4.1 International copyright and design protection

4.1.1 The Berne Convention

The cornerstone of international copyright protection is the Berne Convention. Its latest version was enacted in Paris in 1971. The Berne Convention provides that certain works that primarily fall within the definition of "literary and artistic" must be protected as copyright works. The Convention provides an extensive definition of what is a literary and artistic work. The definition includes many things which in some jurisdictions might be classified separately from artistic and literary works such as musical works. Artistic and literary works include:

> every production in the literary, scientific and artistic domain, whatever may be the mode or form of its expression, such as books, pamphlets and other writings; lectures, addresses, sermons and other works of the same nature; dramatic or dramatico-musical works; choreographic works and

entertainments in dumb show; musical compositions with or without words; cinematographic works to which are assimilated works expressed by a process analogous to cinematography; works of drawing, painting, architecture, sculpture, engraving and lithography; photographic works to which are assimilated works expressed by a process analogous to photography; works of applied art; illustrations, maps, plans, sketches and three-dimensional works relative to geography, topography, architecture or science.[136]

What amounts to a literary and artistic work although extensive also may have limits.[137] These include official texts of a legislative, administrative and legal nature, and official translations of such texts.[138] Members are free to decide the extent to which they will protect works of applied art and industrial designs and models as copyright works.[139]

The Berne Convention also provides that members must ensure copyright owners have certain economic rights – in particular, that of reproduction.[140] It prescribes other economic rights in relation to the communication of copyright works.[141] The *US – 110(5)* dispute at the WTO, discussed above, considered these rights and their relationship with Article 13 of the TRIPS Agreement.[142] Aspects of the communication rights found in the Berne Convention and incorporated into the TRIPS Agreement were the substantive violation of the TRIPS Agreement at issue.[143] Once a right is violated whether the relevant activity falls under the three-step test exception became the core of the dispute. The WTO panel found that what was known as the United States' law's "homestyle exemption" was consistent with Berne Convention rights because it complied with the three-step test, but the "business exemption" was not compliant with that test and so was in violation of the Berne Convention rights.[144]

---

136 Berne Convention, Article 2(1).

137 Berne Convention, Article 2(1).

138 Berne Convention, Article 2(4).

139 Berne Convention, Article 2(7).

140 Berne Convention, Article 9(1). However, the Convention does not expressly state this, rather implying it through its allowance of exceptions to reproduction. Consequently, the scope of the reproduction right is less than clear. For a discussion of the reproduction right under the Berne Convention see J. Ginsburg and S. Ricketson, *International Copyright and Neighbouring Rights: The Berne Convention and Beyond*, above note 36.

141 Berne Convention, Articles 11, 11*bis* and 11*ter*.

142 For discussion of the three-step test see Section [3.6].

143 At issue were Berne Convention, Article 11*bis*(1)(ii) and 11(1)(iii) as incorporated into the TRIPS Agreement, Article 9(1).

144 Berne Convention, Article 11*bis*(1)(ii) and (iii).

The technological limitations of these provisions and their incongruity with the digital world led to the 1996 WCT, discussed below.

The substantive law protection provisions of the Paris Act, of the Berne Convention, with the exception of those relating to moral rights, are imported into the TRIPS Agreement. Article 9 of the TRIPS Agreement provides:

> Members shall comply with Articles 1 through 21 of the Berne Convention (1971) and the Appendix thereto. However, Members shall not have rights or obligations under this Agreement in respect of the rights conferred under Article 6bis of that Convention or of the rights derived therefrom.

4.1.2   The TRIPS Agreement and copyright

The TRIPS Agreement incorporates the substantive provisions of the Berne Convention and uses them as the basis of copyright protection.[145] In addition TRIPS codifies the "idea-expression dichotomy" of copyright. This dichotomy is found in one form or another in many common law countries. It is formally contained in certain statutes such as section 102(b) of the United States Copyright Act. That provision inspired the drafters of Article 9(2) of the TRIPS Agreement, which provides:

> Copyright protection shall extend to expression and not to ideas, procedures, methods of operation or mathematical concepts as such.[146]

In addition to the Berne Convention protection, the TRIPS Agreement provides that members shall provide protection for:

- Computer programs as literary works.[147] Prior to TRIPS some countries had begun to protect computer programs in this way.[148]
- Databases that amount to intellectual creations.[149] This means that countries do not have to protect through copyright databases which are the product of labour ("sweat of the brow") or financial investment even if that labour or investment is substantial.

---

145   TRIPS Agreement, Article 9(1).

146   TRIPS Agreement, Article 9(2).

147   TRIPS Agreement, Article 10(1).

148   Computer programs are also protected as patents in some jurisdictions such as the United States and Australia. They are excluded from patentability as such in the European Union and in New Zealand.

149   TRIPS Agreement, Article 10(2).

They may of course provide another sort of protection for such databases as the European Union has.[150]

- Rental rights in respect of computer programs and films.[151] These rights are often embedded in national law as connected to the right to issue to the public or first distribution. This is particularly so in countries that have inherited and adapted English law. It is important, however, to appreciate the independence of the rental right requirement such that, for example, even where parallel imports (whether online or hard copies) of computer programs and films are permitted these imported copies are sometimes still subject to rental rights. In other words, in some jurisdictions, imported copies cannot be rented without permission of the right holder.

- Performers to prevent unauthorized fixation of their performances and the reproductions of such fixations and to give them control over the communication to the public of their performance.[152]

- Producers of phonograms to prohibit reproduction and rental of their phonograms.[153]

- Broadcasters to prohibit fixation, reproduction of fixations and rebroadcasting, and to give them control over communication to the public of broadcasts.[154]

4.1.3   Other copyright instruments

The Universal Copyright Convention

For a number of years the Universal Copyright Convention (UCC) was important particularly because the United States did not belong to the Berne Convention. The significance of the UCC declined when the United States joined the Berne Convention in 1988. In addition since the emergence of the TRIPS Agreement, the status of the UCC is much diminished and it is for all practical purposes defunct.[155]

---

150   This may raise issues as to whether that *sui generis* protection needs to be applied on a national treatment basis. The European Union applies reciprocity (they only extend this *sui generis* right to those who also provide it) rather than national treatment. See discussion of national treatment in Section [3.4].

151   TRIPS Agreement, Article 11. However, in respect of films it is not obligatory to provide the rental right unless rental has led to widespread copying. In respect of computer programs, the rental right does not apply to rental rights where the program is "not the essential object of the rental".

152   TRIPS Agreement, Article 14(1).

153   TRIPS Agreement, Article 14(2).

154   TRIPS Agreement, Article 14(3).

155   Cambodia and Laos remain members of the Universal Copyright Convention but not the Berne Convention.

The Rome Convention 1961 and Phonograms Convention 1971

The Rome Convention for the Protection of Performers, Producers of Phonograms and Broadcasting Organizations of 1961 provides:

- Protection for performers to prevent the unauthorized fixation of their performances and the reproduction of such fixations.
- Protection for producers of phonograms (often referred to as sound recordings) and the right to prevent reproduction of their phonograms.
- Protection for broadcasters and the right to prevent reproduction of their broadcasts.
- A right to remuneration when sound recordings are broadcast, to be paid to the producer, the performer or both.

Attempts were made in the 1970s to provide more extensive protection against "music piracy" but this was not successful. As of November 2015, the Rome Convention had 92 Contracting Parties. However, the United States is not a signatory of the Rome Convention, in part because as of 2015 it provides no right (either exclusive or by way of remuneration) for the broadcast of sound recordings. While audio-visual performers are theoretically covered under Rome, they have no rights after having consented to a fixation (for example, once an actor has agreed to appear in a motion picture). Hence the Rome Convention is best seen as an instrument protecting music performers (artists).

In 1971, a specific convention was signed to protect only phonogram producers (not performers or broadcasters). It provides essentially a reproduction right in sound recordings. This Phonograms Convention (also referred to as the Geneva Convention) had 78 member states as of November 2015, including the United States and the United Kingdom.

The TRIPS Agreement is now the leading convention in this area. Protection for broadcasters, performers and producers of phonograms under TRIPS is noted above.

The rights of performers, producers of phonograms, and broadcasters set out in the TRIPS Agreement can be limited in various ways, including exceptions, and reservations that were also permitted under the Rome Convention.[156] Broadly, this allows members to implement

---

156 TRIPS Agreement, Article 14(6).

the protections on the basis of reciprocity rather than national treatment.[157]

4.2   (Industrial) designs

Designs (or "industrial designs") are required to be protected at National law under the Paris Convention, which is discussed more fully in respect of patents and trademarks below. The Convention establishes a "right of priority" (typically six months for designs) in Article 4 (discussed in Section [2.1.1]) and a few additional rules, but the level of protection remains very vague. Article 5*quinquies* only provides that "[i]ndustrial designs shall be protected in all the countries of the Union".

The TRIPS Agreement (Article 25) goes much farther than the Paris Convention. First, it contains an obligation to protect "independently created industrial designs" that are "new or original". This formulation reflects the fact that a number of countries provide copyright-like protection for designs (hence the reference to originality) and others use a patent-like system (hence the reference to novelty). The protection need not extend to "designs dictated essentially by technical or functional considerations", thus allowing WTO members to apply a functionality exclusion (or doctrine) to design protection, limiting protection to certain aesthetic features of an otherwise useful object.

Then Article 26 of the TRIPS Agreement provides that the protection must extend to the "making, selling or importing articles bearing or embodying a design which is a copy, or substantially a copy, of the protected design, when such acts are undertaken for commercial purposes". Exceptions are permitted subject to the three-step test (see Section [3.6] [about the three-step test]). The minimum term of protection available must be ten years, although it may be subject to formalities such as registration, deposit and renewal.

While the substantive law of designs is far from fully harmonized internationally, *applications* to protect designs can be done using The Hague system under The Hague Agreement. The original Agreement dates back to 1925 but it was updated a number of times, including in 1960 and 1999. As of November 2015, it had 64 member states. The

---

157   TRIPS Agreement, Article 14(6).

United States joined with effect from May 2015. The 1999 Act and the 1960 Act are still relevant. Under The Hague system, an international design registration may be obtained only by natural persons and legal persons having an establishment, domicile, nationality or, under the 1999 Act, habitual residence in a Contracting Party to either of the two Acts. International design applications are filed with WIPO, either directly or through the industrial property office of the Contracting Party of origin if the law of that Contracting Party so permits or requires. Each application may include up to one hundred designs, provided they all belong to the same class of the International Classification for Industrial Designs (see the Locarno Classification below). Applicants may choose to file an application in English, French or Spanish. Each Contracting Party designated by the applicant may refuse protection based on substantive requirements in domestic law. If no refusal is notified within the specified timeframe (six or possibly 12 months in certain cases) the international registration has effect as a grant of protection in all designated Contracting Parties. The term of protection is five years, renewable (once or twice depending on the Act to which a state is a party).

There is an international classification system for designs, which makes it easier to describe designs and apply for international protection. This system was established by the 1968 Locarno Agreement, which had 54 member states as of November 2015 (but many key countries were *not* (yet) members, including the United States). The Locarno Agreement establishes the "Locarno Classification", which is a list of 32 classes and 219 subclasses and an alphabetical list of approximately 7,000 types of goods that intellectual property offices for Contracting States use when designs are deposited or registered.

4.3   Copyright developments subsequent to the TRIPS Agreement

4.3.1   The WIPO Copyright Treaty 1996 (WCT)

The WCT exists independently of the Berne Convention and is not incorporated into the TRIPS Agreement.[158] It makes reference to the Berne Convention but has been formulated so that members of Berne

---

158 WCT, above note 66.

can choose whether or not to sign up to it. It is not an amendment of the Berne Convention but is an optional protocol to it.[159]

The WCT entered into force on 6 March 2002. It is directed towards copyright protection in the face of new technologies and provides for a number of new rights, including a broad communication right,[160] which gives copyright owners protection when they "make their works available" in the digitally connected world. Making a work available on digital networks even if no unauthorized reproduction or performance takes place may constitute an infringing act. An agreed statement provides that the mere provision of facilities for communication does not amount to communication as is meant in the WCT or the Berne Convention.[161] This is the international rule that gives scope for intermediaries, such as Internet service providers, to have immunity from liability under some national laws.

The WCT also contains an obligation in respect of technological protection measures (TPM), described as a general obligation to provide "legal protection and effective legal remedies against the circumvention of effective technological measures that are used by authors in connection with the exercise of their rights under this Treaty or the Berne Convention and that restrict acts, in respect of their works, which are not authorized by the authors concerned or permitted by law".[162] The WCT also prohibits the removal or alteration of "rights management information" or RMI, including the name of the author or publisher, the title, and various rights management codes, which may be appended to or embedded in digital files.

The WCT adopts a version of the three-step test for exceptions to the rights.[163] It also provides in an agreed statement between the parties to the treaty that parties are permitted:

> to carry forward and appropriately extend into the digital environment limitations and exceptions in their national laws which have been considered acceptable under the Berne Convention. Similarly, these provisions should

---

159 WCT, Articles 1 and 3.
160 WCT, Article 8.
161 WCT Agreed Statement, Article 8.
162 WCT, Article 11.
163 WCT, Article 10(1).

be understood to permit Contracting Parties to devise new exceptions and limitations that are appropriate in the digital network environment.[164]

The United States,[165] the European Union[166] and Australia[167] among many others have adhered to the WCT and purported to give it effect in their laws. Many FTAs post-TRIPS also require the parties to adhere to the standards of the WCT.

Even though the WCT post-dates the TRIPS Agreement the dispute settlement panel in the *US – 110(5)* dispute considered the agreement. The panel concluded that because most of the parties to the WCT were party to both the TRIPS Agreement and the Berne Convention, the WCT could provide contextual guidance to the issues before the panel under TRIPS.[168]

4.3.2 WIPO Producers of Phonograms and Sound Recordings Treaty 1996 (WPPT)

The WIPO Producers of Phonograms and Sound Recordings Treaty 1996, known as the WPPT,[169] requires the introduction of economic rights for performers and producers of phonograms. The WPPT rights are along the lines of the exclusive rights of copyright in relation to other works. In effect the Treaty provides for a new category of work, the "performance". It also recommends the introduction of moral rights for performers.[170] The use of the term "phonogram" is not intended to limit the rights to old technologies. The term is defined to incorporate modern technologies.[171] Like the WCT it contains obligations concerning TPM and RMI and it also provides for exceptions under a three-step test.[172]

---

164 WCT Agreed Statement, Article 10.

165 Digital Millennium Copyright Act of 1999, 112 Stat. 2860, codified at 17 U.S.C. §§ 512, 1201–1205, 1301–1332 (West 2006).

166 European Parliament and Council Directive, Harmonization of certain aspects of copyright and related rights in the information society, 2001/29/EC, 22 May 2001.

167 Copyright Amendment (Digital Agenda) Act 2000 (Aus.).

168 *US-110(5)*, above note 71, [6.70].

169 WPPT, above note 66.

170 WPPT, Article 5.

171 WPPT, Article 2 states that "phonogram" means the fixation of the sounds of a performance or of other sounds, or of a representation of sounds, other than in the form of a fixation incorporated in a cinematographic or other audiovisual work.

172 WPPT, Article 16.

Unlike the Rome Convention, which allowed reciprocity, the WPPT requires national treatment.[173]

4.3.3   The Beijing Treaty on Audio-visual Performances

In 2012, members of WIPO adopted the Beijing Treaty on Audio-visual Performances.[174] It contains rights for audio-visual performers (especially actors), who had very few rights under the 1961 Rome Convention and the WPPT, which essentially protect music performers. The fact that a treaty increasing the level of protection of intellectual property was adopted in China was seen as a significant development. It grants performers four kinds of economic rights for their fixed (recorded) performances (such as motion pictures): (1) the right of reproduction;[175] (2) the right of distribution;[176] (3) the right of rental;[177] and (4) the right of making available[178] (as in the WCT and WPPT).

As to live performances, the Treaty grants performers: (1) the right of broadcasting (except in the case of rebroadcasting); (2) the right of communication to the public (except where the performance is a broadcast performance); and (3) the right of fixation (anti-bootlegging).[179] The Treaty also grants performers moral rights of attribution and integrity. However, Contracting Parties may limit the right in respect of fixed performances to a right of equitable remuneration. Additionally, Contracting Parties may stipulate in their national laws that once a performer has consented to the audio-visual fixation of a performance, the exclusive rights mentioned above are transferred to the producer. As of November 2015, 10 eligible parties had ratified or acceded to the Beijing Treaty. Thirty eligible parties must adhere (ratify or acede) to the Treaty before it enters into force.[180]

---

173 WPPT, Article 4.

174 Beijing Treaty on Audio-visual Performances, adopted 12 June 2012 (not yet in force), at http://www.wipo.int/wipolex/en/treaties/text.jsp?file_id=295837#art26, last accessed 26 October 2015 (hereinafter Beijing Treaty).

175 Beijing Treaty, Article 7.

176 Beijing Treaty, Article 8.

177 Beijing Treaty, Article 9.

178 Beijing Treaty, Article 10.

179 Beijing Treaty, Article 11.

180 Beijing Treaty, Article 26.

4.3.4 The Marrakesh Treaty to Facilitate Access to Published Works for Persons Who Are Blind, Visually Impaired, or Otherwise Print Disabled

In 2013, under the aegis of WIPO, the Marrakesh Treaty to Facilitate Access to Published Works for Persons Who Are Blind, Visually Impaired, or Otherwise Print Disabled was adopted.[181] It obliges Contracting Parties to introduce a standard set of limitations and exceptions to copyright rules in order to permit reproduction, distribution and making available of published works in formats designed to be accessible to visually impaired users, and to permit exchange of these works across borders by organizations that serve those beneficiaries. Only works "in the form of text, notation and/or related illustrations, whether published or otherwise made publicly available in any media", including audio books, fall within the scope of the treaty.[182] As of November 2015, it had been ratified or adhered to by eleven countries.[183] The Treaty was considered important in part because it was the first instrument adopted with the limited aim of imposing a mandatory limitation on copyright rights.[184]

4.4   International patent protection

4.4.1   General

Until the advent of the TRIPS Agreement, the major international agreement over patents was the Paris Convention. Overall it provided very few details of the substantive law of patents, but was a significant milestone as the first international agreement to provide any standard for patents.[185] The substantive provisions of the Paris Convention are incorporated into the TRIPS Agreement. As well as providing limited substantive law minima, the Paris Convention contains certain provisions that have assisted the international registration of patents.

---

181 Marrakesh Treaty to Facilitate Access to Published Works for Persons Who Are Blind, Visually Impaired, or Otherwise Print Disabled, adopted 27 June 2013, (not yet in force) at http://www.wipo.int/meetings/en/doc_details.jsp?doc_id=245323, accessed 5 November 2015 (hereinafter Marrakesh Visually Impaired Treaty).

182 Marrakesh Visually Impaired Treaty, Article 2.

183 It will enter into force once 20 eligible parties have done so, Marrakesh Visually Impaired Treaty, Article 19.

184 This was also the aim of the Appendix to the Berne Convention, of course, but it was an Appendix to an instrument (Berne) that contains a series of mandatory rights.

185 See Section [2.1.1] for further details.

This system of international patent registration cooperation has been extended in the Patent Cooperation Treaty (PCT). In 2000 the Patent Law Treaty, which provides for further procedural matters, was agreed between some 30 or so WIPO members. There were some discussions at WIPO about a substantive patent law treaty,[186] but a treaty has not eventuated.

4.4.2 Patents and the TRIPS Agreement

Subject matter, exclusive rights and term

The TRIPS Agreement provides substantive standards for patents. Article 27 requires that patent protection be available for inventions in all fields of technology provided that they are new, involve an inventive step, and are capable of industrial application.[187] A footnote deems that inventive step is synonymous with non-obviousness and industrial application is synonymous with usefulness.[188] None of these terms is defined in the Agreement and so members have their own definitions and approaches to these criteria in their laws. This means that the requirement for patents over all subject matter is the minimum standard (but that does not mean everything is patentable). Members have different approaches in particular to inventive step and usefulness resulting in different patent laws around the world.[189] In effect countries can calibrate their definitions of these criteria to suit local needs and development issues. In doing so, however, they must still comply with the TRIPS Agreement.

Article 28 of the TRIPS Agreement provides that patentees must have the exclusive rights of making, using, offering for sale, selling, or importing[190] the patented product and equivalent for patented processes.

---

186 WIPO, Suggestions for the Further Development of the International Patent Law, document SCP/4/2, 25 September 2000, at www.wipo.int/edocs/mdocs/scp/en/scp_4/scp_4_2.pdf, accessed 2 September 2015.

187 TRIPS Agreement, Article 27(1).

188 TRIPS Agreement, Article 27, footnote 5.

189 For a discussion of various utility and industrial applicability standards, see Expert Report of Daniel J. Gervais, *Eli Lilly and Company v Government of Canada* (2015), at http://bit.ly/1QEgUBc, accessed 2 September 2015.

190 TRIPS Agreement, Article 28, footnote 6 provides in relation to importing that "[t]his right, like all other rights conferred under this Agreement in respect of the use, sale, importation or other distribution of goods, is subject to the provisions of Article 6". Article 6 provides that matters

Patent law is premised on a principle that society benefits from the disclosure of inventive activity and that patents are given in exchange for that disclosure.[191] This incentive to disclose must be stronger than the desire to keep the information protected as a trade secret or other form of confidential information. This is sometimes called a social contract. The theory behind patents is, in summary, that the incentive of exclusive rights (the patent) will incentivize and increase investment in research and innovation, especially in areas that involve a high cost of research and low cost to replicate the result, such as many pharmaceutical compounds. In that area the cost of developing and testing may amount to tens or even hundreds of millions of dollars but often the compound can be duplicated for cents.

The TRIPS Agreement outlines that patent systems must require a certain level of disclosure and provides that members shall require that patent applicants "disclose the invention in a manner sufficiently clear and complete for the invention to be carried out by a person skilled in the art and may require the applicant to indicate the best mode for carrying out the invention known to the inventor".[192]

Under the TRIPS Agreement patents are granted for a minimum period of 20 years from when a patent application is filed.[193] Many countries had to extend the term of patents from periods such as 14, 16 or 17 years in order to comply with the TRIPS Agreement. In 2000 the United States brought a dispute against Canada alleging that it was in breach of the TRIPS Agreement term of patent protection.[194] Canada had amended its Patent Act to increase patent protection terms from 17 years from the grant of a patent to 20 years from the application

---

relating to exhaustion of rights cannot be brought to dispute settlement. See parallel importing discussion at Section [5.3].

191   The TRIPS Agreement, Article 39, states that WTO members must in their national law provide private parties the possibility of preventing information lawfully within their control from being disclosed to, acquired by, or used by others without their consent in a manner contrary to honest commercial practices so long as such information: (a) is secret in the sense that it is not, as a body or in the precise configuration and assembly of its components, generally known among or readily accessible to persons within the circles that normally deal with the kind of information in question; (b) has commercial value because it is secret; and (c) has been subject to reasonable steps under the circumstances, by the person lawfully in control of the information, to keep it secret. Compare the definition of "trade secret" in the US Uniform Trade Secrets Act, which, as of June 2015, had been adopted by 48 US states and the District of Columbia.

192   TRIPS Agreement, Article 29.

193   TRIPS Agreement, Article 33.

194   WTO Panel Report, *Canada – Term of Patent Protection*, WT/DS170/AB/R, (12 October 2000).

for a patent. The new law applied to patents filed after 1 October 1989. Patents filed before that date only had protection for 17 years from the date of grant of the patent. The panel and the Appellate Body found that Canada had infringed the TRIPS Agreement because patents granted within three years of 1989 would expire before the 20 year period.

Limitations, exclusions and exceptions

Members may make exceptions to the requirement to provide for patents in all fields of technology on certain grounds. These include on the basis of *"ordre public* or morality". The provision states that such exclusions can be "to protect human, animal or plant life or health or to avoid serious prejudice to the environment, provided that such exclusion is not made merely because the exploitation is prohibited by their law".[195] The meaning of *ordre public* is any matter which is of fundamental importance to a society. The WTO has not considered the provision in the context of the TRIPS Agreement, but in relation to GATS it has. The WTO's Appellate Body concluded that concept meant "the preservation of the fundamental interests of a society, as reflected in public policy and law".[196] In GATS "public order" rather than *"ordre public"* is used. If anything the TRIPS terminology is wider and so the GATS interpretation is a useful guide.

The TRIPS Agreement also allows exclusions for:

(1) diagnostic, therapeutic and surgical methods for the treatment of humans or animals;
(2) plants and animals other than micro-organisms, and essentially biological processes for the production of plants or animals other than non-biological and microbiological processes.[197]

In relation to (2), if members do exclude plants from patents then the TRIPS Agreement requires protection of plant varieties by a *sui generis* rights regime.[198] Members must protect plant varieties either through a *sui generis* system or patents.

---

195 TRIPS Agreement, Article 27(2).

196 See WTO Appellate Body Report, *United States – Measures Affecting the Cross-border Supply of Gambling and Betting Services*, WT/DS285/AB/R, (7 April 2005); see also WTO Decision by the Arbitrator, *Recourse to Arbitration by the United States under Article 22.6 of the DSU*, WT/DS285/ARB, (21 December 2007).

197 TRIPS Agreement, Article 27(3).

198 TRIPS Agreement, Article 27(3)(b).

In addition to these exceptions, Article 30 of the TRIPS Agreement provides the three-step test under which other exceptions to patent protection may be made.[199] The most common of such exceptions are ones relating to regulatory review of patented products and experimental use of patents.

Article 30 was the subject of a complaint brought by the European Union against two exceptions to a patent holder's exclusive rights to make and use under Canada's law.[200] The Canadian Patent Act included a regulatory review exception that allowed parties other than the patent holder to make patented products (namely pharmaceuticals) and to apply for regulatory approval for the marketing during the patent term. Related to the regulatory review exception was a stockpiling exception that allowed producers (who also utilized the regulatory review exception) other than the patent owner to make patented products and store them until the patent had expired.

The European Communities alleged that both of these exceptions breached patent holders' exclusive rights to make, use and sell a patent under Article 28(1) and that they fell foul of the requirement in Article 27 for there to be no discrimination between fields of technology. Canada argued that the exceptions were permitted under Article 30. It also argued that the no discrimination part of Article 27 did not apply to Article 30 exceptions. The panel found that Article 30 was met for the regulatory review exception but not the stockpiling exception. The panel found that the stockpiling exception failed the first step of the three-step test in that it was not limited enough.[201] On the contrary, the regulatory review exception was more limited in its scope and it did not conflict with the normal exploitation of the patentee (Article 30, second step) or the legitimate expectations of the patentee (Article 30, third step).

The panel found that Article 27 of the TRIPS Agreement was relevant to the interpretation of Article 30 and required that the exception did not discriminate between fields of technology. As written, the Canadian law exception could apply to other technologies but the detailed regulations that had so far been made under the law only

---

199 See discussion of the three-step test in Section [3.6].

200 *Canada Pharmaceuticals*, above note 115. Third parties included Australia, Brazil, Colombia, Cuba, India, Israel, Japan, Poland, Switzerland, Thailand and the United States.

201 See discussion of the three-step test in Section [3.6.2].

applied to pharmaceuticals. The panel absorbed itself in a discussion of *de jure* and *de facto* discrimination and found the regulatory review exception was neither. From a VCLT interpretation perspective, Article 27 is relevant "context". However, creating a direct applicability as the panel did was arguably not a necessary approach based on both the wording of the TRIPS Agreement and the object and purpose of Article 30. This is particularly because the best way to limit an exception is to limit its applicability to the particular field or sector that needs the exception.[202] The panel stated:

> An Article 30 exception cannot be made limited by limiting it to one field of technology, because the effects of each exception must be found to be "limited" when measured against each affected patent. Beyond that it is not true that Article 27 requires all Article 30 exceptions to be applied to all products.[203]

This dispute never went to the Appellate Body. The panel did not apply Articles 7 and 8 of the TRIPS Agreement to interpret the provision. They noted that Articles 7 and 8 should not make the rest of the Agreement ineffective. That is correct but they are important interpretative tools and it was difficult to see how if at all the panel took the principles into account.[204]

Article 31 of the TRIPS Agreement provides the framework for compulsory licensing of patents. It is perhaps best known for its application to the manufacture of pharmaceuticals in national-emergency situations, but it has wider application.[205] It applies to any authorization of use of a patent, under certain conditions.[206] These conditions include that "the scope and duration of such use shall be limited to the purpose for which it was authorized".[207] Also, the patentee must be paid an

---

202 For a discussion of this difficulty, see G. B. Dinwoodie and R. Dreyfuss, "Diversifying Without Discrimination Complying with the Mandate of the TRIPS Agreement", 13 *Michigan Telecomm Tech L Rev* (2007), 445.

203 *Canada Pharmaceuticals*, above note 115, at [7.92].

204 See discussion of treaty interpretation in Section [3.2].

205 TRIPS Agreement, Article 31(a). See discussion in Section [5.3.3] about Article 31*bis* and parallel importing of pharmaceuticals made under compulsory license.

206 TRIPS Agreement, Article 31(b) waives the requirement that reasonable efforts be made to consult with the patentee in situations of national emergency. This leaves open the possibility for other compulsory license situations in which "the proposed user has made efforts to obtain authorization from the right holder on reasonable commercial terms and conditions and that such efforts have not been successful within a reasonable period of time".

207 TRIPS Agreement, Article 31(c).

"adequate remuneration in the circumstances of each case, taking into account the economic value of the authorization".[208]

Under the Paris Convention a member was permitted to issue a compulsory license to "work" a patent in its local territory. The extent of a nation's power to require working of a patent was much debated during negotiation of the TRIPS Agreement and that negotiating history lies behind Article 31. Not insignificantly, however, Article 5 of the Paris Convention is also incorporated in the TRIPS Agreement,[209] and so the interpretation of that Article and Article 31 must be consistent. Thus, if a working requirement is made it must meet the terms of Article 31. Arguably, however, the TRIPS Agreement recognizes that imports can substitute for local working. Such an interpretation is consistent with the trade-related goals of the TRIPS Agreement. It is not, however, wholly consistent with the inclusion of Article 5 of the Paris Convention. Because of its inclusion Article 5 must be interpreted to have some meaning.

Working requirements remain controversial. If imports are not an adequate substitute for working because they are not available in a real sense or even a practical sense (because they are not affordable), then issues arise as to whether a local working requirement can substitute for non-supply or even parallel importing. Some countries have exceptions relating to when a market is not supplied.

Confidential information

Inventors and companies often have to decide whether to apply for a patent, which in most cases implies a public disclosure even before a decision is made to grant the patent.[210] If the patent is granted, it may be that the claims can fairly easily be circumvented (legally) by a competitor. Then there are significant costs associated with patent applications. Finally, some information while valuable is simply not patentable (a list of customers for example). Companies may opt to protect this type of information under laws concerning trade secrets and confidential information.

There are a number of international rules that are relevant in this area, though not a comprehensive set. This is partly because the area is

---

208   TRIPS Agreement, Article 31(h).
209   TRIPS Agreement, Article 2(1).
210   Typically, patent applications are published 18 months after filing.

often regulated under general principles of laws of unfair competition, theft and, in the United States, state trade secret legislation – most states reflect the Uniform Trade Secrets Act and as such are difficult to harmonize.

The Paris Convention only contains a general prohibition against "[a]ny act of competition contrary to honest practices in industrial or commercial matters".[211] The TRIPS Agreement "unpacked" this prohibition by adding more specific protection of "undisclosed information" and "data submitted to governments or governmental agencies".[212]

With respect to confidential information, the TRIPS Agreement states that WTO members must provide private parties "the possibility of preventing information lawfully within their control from being disclosed to, acquired by, or used by others without their consent in a manner contrary to honest commercial practices" subject to three conditions, namely that said information:

> (a) is secret in the sense that it is not, as a body or in the precise configuration and assembly of its components, generally known among or readily accessible to persons within the circles that normally deal with the kind of information in question;
> (b) has commercial value because it is secret; and
> (c) has been subject to reasonable steps under the circumstances, by the person lawfully in control of the information, to keep it secret.[213]

A separate issue is the disclosure of information submitted to governmental authorities to obtain marketing approval. Pharmaceutical companies submit clinical and other data and often want legal means to prevent its disclosure to the public. They also want a right to prevent the simple reliance on such data at the expiration of a patent by competitors wishing to commercialize a "generic", same compound or biosimilar version of the pharmaceutical product. The TRIPS Agreement contains an obligation to protect some data against disclosure (unless disclosure is necessary to protect the public) and "unfair commercial use" (undefined): when the data concern new chemical entities, and provided the origination of the data involved "a considerable effort".[214]

---

211 Paris Convention, Article 10*bis*(2).
212 TRIPS Agreement, Article 39(1).
213 TRIPS Agreement, Article 39(2).
214 TRIPS Agreement, Article 39(3).

No specific term of protection is provided. Trade agreements negotiated since the TRIPS Agreement (discussed below[215]) have tended to include a minimum term for at least the latter type of data (submitted for regulatory approval) and a more specific definition of the types of "unfair" uses that are prohibited. The recently concluded text of the IP Chapter of the Trans-pacific Partnership (TPP) is a TRIPS-plus step in that regard.

Special patent-related provisions for developing countries

In relation to patents, in particular, the TRIPS Agreement provides a number of transitional arrangements for developing countries. Developing countries were entitled to a four-year delay to comply with TRIPS.[216] The principles of national treatment and MFN, however, applies during that period.[217] Least developed countries were allowed an original transitional period of 11 years, which has been extended to last until the end of 2033.[218] As this time nears end controversial negotiations are underway for further extension. Under the Doha Declaration on the TRIPS Agreement and Public Health,[219] for pharmaceutical-related patents, a separate extension is in place until 2016.

At the time of signing of the TRIPS Agreement, where product patents related to technologies were not protected in a developing country, a further five-year compliance delay was permissible.[220] If a developing country made use of these delay periods in relation to patents for pharmaceuticals and agricultural chemical products TRIPS imposed certain conditions. Countries utilizing the delay were obliged to provide a means so that the patents could still be filed. This was, and is, known as "the mailbox system". One of the countries that took advantage of this was India because at the time of entry into the TRIPS Agreement India did not allow for the patenting of pharmaceutical products. They did, however, patent pharmaceutical processes.

---

215 See Section [5.6].

216 No member was required to comply with TRIPS until one year after its entry into force: TRIPS Agreement, Article 65(1).

217 TRIPS Agreement, Article 65(2). Under Article 65(3) any other member in transition from a centrally planned to a free enterprise economy could also make use of the delay period.

218 *Extension of the Transition Period under Article 66.1 for Least-Developed Country Members*, 6 November 2013 (Decision of the TRIPS Council).

219 WTO, "Developing countries' transition periods", www.wto.org/english/tratop_e/trips_e/factsheet_pharm04_e.htm, accessed 17 April 2015.

220 TRIPS Agreement, Article 65(4).

The United States and the European Union (then European Communities) brought a dispute over India's mailbox system.[221] The complainant alleged that India did not have an adequate mailbox system for patent applications, and in particular this inadequacy was revealed because the Indian law both lacked transparency and had failed to ensure future marketing rights for patent owners. India had put into place various "executive law" measures, in order to comply with the TRIPS Agreement. In essence the complainant alleged that India's Parliament ought to have enacted these measures so they could not be overruled in a court. India was found to be in breach of TRIPS.

The matter went to the WTO Appellate Body where India was found to be in breach of the transitional requirements of the TRIPS Agreement.[222]

4.4.3   The Paris Convention

The Paris Convention is not primarily a minimum standards substantive rights treaty.[223] It provides important norms in relation to priority dates[224] and international recognition of such dates and related matters to smooth international registration. A key provision is the requirement of national treatment for patent owners.[225] As noted above, key parts of the Convention are incorporated into the TRIPS Agreement.

The Paris Convention also provides that a patent in one member country is independent from a patent in another member country.[226] The effect of this is that if a patent application is successful in one country that does not mean it will be automatically registered in another country. Similarly, if a patent is rejected that alone should not prevent registration in another country. In other words a patent application has to meet the requirements of the law of

---

221 WTO Panel Report, *India – Patent Protection for Pharmaceutical and Agricultural Chemical Products*, WT/DS79/R (24 August 1998).

222 WTO Appellate Body Report, *India – Patent Protection for Pharmaceutical and Agricultural Chemical Products*, WT/DS50/AB/R (19 December 1997).

223 See the discussion in Section [2.1.1]. Compare the Berne Convention, for example, which provides substantive rights for copyright protection.

224 Paris Convention, Articles 4A–4C.

225 Paris Convention, Article 2(1).

226 Paris Convention, Article 4*bis*.

the country in which registration is sought if it is to be registered there.[227]

4.4.4 The Patent Cooperation Treaty (PCT)[228]

The PCT, to which there are 147 Contracting States, is a special agreement open to membership by Paris Convention members.[229] The 12-month priority period of the Paris Convention, under the PCT, can be extended de pacto for as long as 30 months in order that an applicant can obtain further information on prior art. The overall framework of the PCT is to provide procedures for the initial stages of making a patent application. The Patent Law Treaty (which has a considerably smaller membership) expands on some of these procedures.[230]

4.4.5 The International Union for the Protection of New Varieties of Plants

As the TRIPS Agreement included a requirement for the protection of plant varieties or plant breeders' rights, the International Union for the Protection of New Varieties of Plants 1961 (UPOV) has received more attention.

There are three main Acts of the UPOV Convention still relevant today, adopted in 1972 (essentially similar to the 1961 Convention in substance), 1978 and 1991, respectively. As of March 2015, only Belgium is still party only to the 1961/1972 Convention. Of the 71 other members of UPOV, which include the African Intellectual Property Organization and the European Union, 17 are party to the 1978 Act. All others are party to the most recent 1991 Act.

Essentially, UPOV seeks to encourage the development of new plant varieties on the basis that protecting new varieties acts as an incentive to plant breeders to continue development. By promoting international harmonization and cooperation between its members, registration and

---

227 Differences in national patent laws have led to an ongoing and, at the time of writing, still unsuccessful attempt to harmonize patent law further. See Draft Substantive Patent Law Treaty discussion on WIPO's website, www.wipo.int/patent-law/en/draft_splt.htm, accessed 26 October 2015.

228 Patent Cooperation Treaty, 1 April 2002, at http://www.wipo.int/pct/en/texts/articles/atoc.htm, accessed 26 October 2015, (hereinafter PCT).

229 Paris Convention, Article 9.

230 This treaty was negotiated after the TRIPS Agreement in 2000. Attempts at WIPO for a subsequent Substantive Patent Law Treaty have not progressed to completion.

protection of new plant varieties can be obtained with minimal cost.[231] This is in line with the TRIPS Agreement's goal to provide protection for plant varieties.[232] TRIPS does not require that WTO members select the 1978 or 1991 Act. The 1991 Act is stronger than the 1978 version and often described as providing "patent-like" protection. It does allow UPOV members to provide that farmers can keep seeds and other propagation material from protected varieties for use on their own farms (the so-called "farmers" privilege), but it is not a right, unlike under the 1978 Act.

Many countries that recognize plant breeders' rights also grant patents on plants, especially those that have been genetically modified. The United States provides breeders' rights, standard (utility) patents and a specific form of plant patent. Plant patents are for asexually reproduced novel plants.

4.4.6   The Convention on Biological Diversity 1992 and the Nagoya Protocol

This Agreement is not a patent law treaty, but as its name suggests it is about biodiversity. The relationship between the CBD and the TRIPS Agreement has been discussed at the WTO in connection with a review of Article 27(3) of the TRIPS Agreement. That Article allows for exceptions from patents but requires protection of plant varieties under either a patent or a *sui generis* system, such as UPOV described above.[233] The main aims of the CBD include:

- to conserve biological diversity;
- to ensure sustainable use of biological resources; and
- to fairly share benefits arising from utilization of genetic resources.[234]

The relationship between these goals, patents to exploit plants, plant variety rights and also the connection with claims for the protection of traditional knowledge remain live issues. The Nagoya Protocol is discussed further below. It, in particular, relates to the connection

---

231 International Union for the Protection of New Varieties of Plants, *What It Is, What It Does*, at www.upov.int/export/sites/upov/about/en/pdf/pub437.pdf, accessed 26 October 2015.

232 See TRIPS Agreement, Article 27(3)(b).

233 This review has also made a connection with the debate over traditional knowledge which is discussed at Section [5.5].

234 CBD, Article 1.

between the CBD and the protection of traditional knowledge, discussed below in Section [5.5].

The proposal that has been most discussed in the TRIPS Council would require that patent applications, which relate to an invention that makes use of biological and genetic resources, must disclose that use.[235] At the time of writing this discussion is not progressing and the likely outcome of this discussion is that there will not be any amendment of the TRIPS Agreement to incorporate a disclosure requirement of this sort in the foreseeable future.

4.5   Trademarks, unfair competition and GIs protection

Trademark law (and the related laws of unfair competition and GIs protection) in the international context is a prime example of what the future of international intellectual property is likely to debate and negotiate about. Trademarks – along with patents – are some of the quintessential developed-country intellectual property types. While businesses count on their trademarks to distinguish their products from the products of other businesses, often contravening interests are in play.

At the time of writing, a hot-button issue that exemplifies this dilemma is plain packaging of tobacco. It is widely agreed upon that tobacco is harmful to human health. The WHO maintains that tobacco use is "one of the biggest threats the world has ever faced".[236] Australia enacted plain packaging regulations for tobacco products, which mandated that tobacco products be sold in packets of a specified colour and without graphic logos including where they are trademarks. In addition the legislation requires that the word trademark (brand name of the tobacco) can only appear in a standard font form in a prescribed place on the packaging.[237]

Major producers of tobacco, including the Dominican Republic, Honduras, Ukraine and Nicaragua, filed a complaint with the WTO in

---

235 See generally WTO "TRIPS: Reviews, Article 27.3(b) and Related Issues" (2008) World Trade Organization, www.wto.org/english/tratop_e/trips_e/art27_3b_e.htm, accessed 26 October 2015.

236 World Health Organization, (updated July 2015) "Tobacco Fact Sheet", at www.who.int/media-centre/factsheets/fs339/en/index.html, accessed 26 October 2015.

237 See Tobacco Plain Packaging Act 2011 (Cth) (Australia); Tobacco Plain Packaging Regulations 2011 (Cth) (Australia).

opposition to Australia's actions.[238] It is plain to see that the interests of public health and the intellectual property interests of tobacco producers diverge. Hence, the interplay between the TRIPS Agreement and the Paris Convention, and both trademark and unfair competition law, with the interests of WHO members who wish to introduce plain packaging as suggested in the Framework Convention on Tobacco Control Guidelines is at the very centre of this dispute.[239] This debate is certain to continue.

4.5.1   The TRIPS Agreement and trademarks

The TRIPS Agreement sets minimum standards for protection of trademarks and GIs. In relation to trademarks it provides:

> Any sign, or combination of signs, capable of distinguishing goods or services of one undertaking from those of other undertakings, shall be capable of constituting a trademark. Such signs, in particular words including personal names, letters, numerals, figurative elements and combinations of colours as well as any combination of such signs, shall be eligible for registration as trademarks. Where signs are not inherently capable of distinguishing the relevant goods or services, Members may make registrability depend on distinctiveness acquired through use. Members may require, as a condition of registration, that signs be visually perceptible.[240]

The effect of the last sentence is that only those members who choose to do so provide for sound, smell and taste signs as trademarks. In the WTO dispute concerning the use of Cuban trademarks, *Havana Club*, the panel concluded that Article 15 of the TRIPS Agreement did not apply to trade names. The Appellate Body reversed this decision and said that if the negotiators had meant to exclude trade names there would have been no reason to incorporate Article 8 of the Paris Convention, which protects trade names, into the TRIPS Agreement.[241]

---

238 WTO, Request for Consultations by the Dominican Republic, *Australia – Certain Measures Concerning Trademarks, Geographical Indications and Other Plain Packaging Requirements Applicable to Tobacco Products and Packaging*, WT/DS441/1, 23 July 2012.

239 Guidelines for Implementation of Article 11 of the WHO Framework Convention on Tobacco Control (Packaging and Labelling of Tobacco Products), 22 November 2008, FCTC/COP3(10), Art. 46.

240 TRIPS Agreement, Article 15(1).

241 WTO Appellate Body Report, *US – Section 211 Omnibus Appropriations Act of 1998*, WT/DS176/AB/R (2 January 2002), at [338].

The owner of a trademark is to be given certain exclusive rights:

> to prevent all third parties not having the owner's consent from using in the course of trade identical or similar signs for goods or services which are identical or similar to those in respect of which the trademark is registered where such use would result in a likelihood of confusion. In the case of the use of an identical sign for identical goods or services, a likelihood of confusion shall be presumed.[242]

Further exclusive rights must be provided for well-known marks.[243] Well-known marks relating to goods already received protection under the Paris Convention and the TRIPS Agreement extended this protection to services. The TRIPS Agreement also extended the exclusive rights of the owner of well-known marks to the use of the mark in relation to dissimilar goods or services where that use would be likely to cause confusion or deception.[244] Some jurisdictions have specific well-known marks legislation and other jurisdictions may offer this protection by other legal means, such as passing off. Some members of WIPO adhere to the Joint Recommendation on Well-Known Marks,[245] which details protection. This joint recommendation has also been incorporated into some FTAs.

Additionally, the TRIPS Agreement provides for exceptions to trademark law, "such as fair use of descriptive terms".[246] The trademark provision allowing for exceptions is related to the three-step test, although it only incorporates two steps.[247] This was discussed at the WTO in the dispute brought by the United States against aspects of the European Union's (then European Communities) registration system.[248] Much of the dispute concerned violation of the national treatment principle.[249] Such a violation could potentially be "excused" if it was in compliance with Article 17, but that was not the outcome

---

242 TRIPS Agreement, Article 16(1).

243 TRIPS Agreement, Article 16(2).

244 TRIPS Agreement, Article 16.3 references the Paris Convention, Article 6bis.

245 WIPO, *Joint Recommendation Concerning Provisions on the Protection of Well-Known Mark* (2000), at http://www.wipo.int/edocs/pubdocs/en/marks/833/pub833.pdf, accessed 15 November 2015.

246 TRIPS Agreement, Article 17.

247 See discussion in Section [3.6].

248 WTO Panel Report, *European Communities – Protection of Trademarks and Geographical Indications for Agricultural Products and Foodstuffs*, WT/DS174/R, (15 March 2005). See also discussion in Section [3.6.2].

249 *Ibid.*, at [7.431].

of the dispute. On the facts of the particular dispute, the European Communities were able to use Article 17 to allow for limitations on trademarks existing before the GIs regime came into effect, but not otherwise.[250]

In the area of GIs, the TRIPS Agreement does three main things. First, it creates a dual layer of protection for GIs. The first layer obligates WTO members to "provide the legal means for interested parties to prevent (a) the use of any means in the designation or presentation of a good that indicates or suggests that the good in question originates in a geographical area other than the true place of origin in a manner which misleads the public as to the geographical origin of the good".[251] The second layer protects against the use of a geographical indication identifying wines and spirits "even where the true origin of the goods is indicated or the geographical indication is used in translation or accompanied by expressions such as 'kind', 'type', 'style', 'imitation' or the like".[252] In other words, it protects beyond (traditional) trademark law. Second, the TRIPS Agreement provides a set of detailed rules for the interaction between GIs and (other) trademarks. Third, the TRIPS Agreement obligates WTO members to negotiate the establishment of a GI registration and notification system, and they have been at it since 1995.[253] Yet no significant progress has been made on the register, despite the renewed push contained in the 2001 Doha Declaration.[254] Part of the issue is that the WTO members who are pushing for international protection of GIs disagree on the scope and purpose of their effort. The European Union's focus has been on the establishment of the TRIPS Article 23(4) register. Other WTO members, many of them developing countries, have insisted on an extension of the higher level of protection contained in Article 23(1) of the TRIPS Agreement to products other than wines and spirits.[255] They consider the emphasis in TRIPS on alcoholic beverages to be both culturally discriminatory and a commercial impediment to the ability

---

250 *Ibid.*, at [7.655]–[7.661].

251 TRIPS Agreement, Article 22(2).

252 TRIPS Agreement, Article 23(1).

253 See D. Gervais, *The TRIPS Agreement: Drafting History and Analysis*, above note 98, at 100–126.

254 World Trade Organization, Ministerial Declaration, WT/MIN(01)/DEC1, (20 November 2001), at [18].

255 For a discussion of Asian countries' positions, see Min-Chiuan Wang, "The Asian Consciousness and Interests in Geographical Indications", 96 *The Trademark Reporter*, (2006), 939–940.

to collect potentially higher rents associated with GIs on other types of products protected.[256]

4.5.2   The Paris Convention

Trademark protection

The Paris Convention deals with a number of important procedural matters, including the right of priority.[257]

The few substantive law provisions relate to the protection of well-known marks and protection of state emblems, official hallmarks and the like.[258] The Paris Convention requires national treatment in relation to trademarks owned by foreigners.[259] It also affirms the independence of registration of same or similar trademarks in different territories. The principle of independence has the effect that registration cannot be refused or invalidated in one territory only on the basis that registration has not occurred in the country of origin of the trademark or any other territory.[260]

Trademarks covered by the Paris Convention may only be denied registration or invalidated when they are:

- of such a nature as to infringe rights acquired by third parties in the country where protection is claimed (that is, someone in the target country is already using the mark);
- devoid of any distinctive character, or consist exclusively of signs or indications which may serve, in trade, to designate the kind, quality, quantity, intended purpose, value, place of origin, of the goods, or the time of production, or have become customary in the current language or in the bona fide and established practices of the trade of the country where protection is claimed; this may vary from country to country, in part because of linguistic differences. For example, a trademark may be registered in respect

---

256 See T. Dromard, "Le champagne en quête de nouvelles terres", *Le Figaro*, 26 October 2007, http://avis-vin.lefigaro.fr/magazine-vin/08920-le-champagne-en-quete-de-nouvelles-terres, accessed 22 April 2015. According to this article, the price of a hectare of land (approximately 2.5 acres) moving from outside to inside the appellation zone would jump by 30,000 per cent to almost $1,200,000.

257 Paris Convention, Articles 4A and 4C. See also discussion in Section [2.1.1].

258 Paris Convention, Article 6*ter*. See also discussion in Section [2.1.1].

259 Paris Convention, Article 2(1).

260 Paris Convention, Article 6.

of a pharmaceutical product not yet approved for sale. As it stands, however, the article does not apply to renewals, however;

• contrary to morality or public order and, in particular, of such a nature as to deceive the public. This will also vary from country to country.[261]

A further limitation is provided by Article 10*bis* (discussed below), which, like most substantive provisions of the Paris Convention, was incorporated into the TRIPS Agreement and imposes fairly broad rules on unfair competition.

The Paris Convention also provides that the nature of goods to which a trademark is applied must not form an obstacle to registration of the trademark.[262] The limitations described above contained in Article 6 *quinquies* B[263] are subject to Article 10*bis*, which deals with unfair competition, the topic of the next section.

Unfair competition

The Paris Convention has a general provision that members must provide protection against unfair competition, as follows:

(1)   The countries of the Union are bound to assure to nationals of such countries effective protection against unfair competition.

(2)   Any act of competition contrary to honest practices in industrial or commercial matters constitutes an act of unfair competition.

(3)   The following in particular shall be prohibited:

   (i)   all acts of such a nature as to create confusion by any means whatever with the establishment, the goods, or the industrial or commercial activities, of a competitor;

   (ii)   false allegations in the course of trade of such a nature as to discredit the establishment, the goods, or the industrial or commercial activities, of a competitor;

   (iii)   indications or allegations the use of which in the course of trade is liable to mislead the public as to the nature, the manufacturing process, the characteristics, the suitability for their purpose, or the quantity, of the goods.[264]

---

261   Paris Convention, Article 6*quinquies* B.

262   Paris Convention, Article 7.

263   See above note 261.

264   Paris Convention, Article 10*bis*.

There is no generally accepted definition as to what amounts to unfair competition law. Indeed, it is widely recognized that what civil lawyers call unfair competition may be much broader than the common law perception of what amounts to unfair competition. Interestingly, the phrase is not repeated in the TRIPS Agreement. As discussed above, TRIPS (Article 39) expanded the obligation in respect of undisclosed information and data submitted to obtain regulatory approval.[265]

4.5.3   The Nice Agreement on the Classification of Goods and Services 1957[266]

It would be difficult, if not impossible, to coordinate international registration unless similar categories of goods or services were used by all trademark registries. Trade and service marks are registered in respect of a class of goods or services and the scope of the registration usually only extends to those goods or services or ones similar to them. The Nice Agreement on the Classification of Goods and Services provides a standard for classification of goods and services and is used by many countries whether they are signatories or not.

4.5.4   The Madrid Agreement and Protocol

Members of the Paris Convention can become a member of either or both the Madrid Agreement or Protocol. WIPO's Madrid system is not an international trademark registration, but it is the nearest approximation in view of the territoriality of trademarks because it provides for the use of one international trademark application to be made rather than multiple national applications. The applicant nominates the countries in which registration is sought in the application, which is examined by a designated registration office and is either accepted or refused. Whatever the outcome of the application, the International Bureau, the administrative wing of WIPO, must be notified, after which the Bureau in turn notifies registries in the designated countries. The trademark can be accepted in the designated countries without further examination, thereby providing one of the major advantages of the Madrid system for trademark applicants.

---

265 D. Gervais, The TRIPS Agreement: Drafting History and Analysis, above note 98, at 541–546.

266 See Nice Agreement Concerning the International Classification of Goods and Services for the Purposes of the Registration of Marks 1957, at www.wipo.int/treaties/en/classification/nice/trtdocs_wo019.html, accessed 10 July 2013.

Under the Madrid Agreement an international application can be made once a first registration is completed in one member country. Conversely, under the Madrid Protocol an international application can be made when a first application in a member country has been made. The Madrid system has a number of safeguards, including "dependence on the basic mark" for five years. If a trademark is revoked in the office of origin, for example, the international application and the trademarks registered in designated countries must also be revoked. After five years all the trademark registrations become independent.

4.5.5   The Lisbon system

In 1958, a new international register was set up for appellations of origin (AOs). These appellations are often used in connection with beer, wine and spirits to identify a country, region or locality which serves to designate a product originating therein, the quality or characteristics of which are due exclusively or essentially to the geographical environment, including natural and human factors. While alcoholic products are the main category of products for which AOs have traditionally been used internationally, AOs can be used for any other product, including coffee, tea, cigars, cheese, crafts and mineral water. AOs are not like normal trademarks though they can be, and often are, used in conjunction with such marks. For example, Champagne is an AO that is generally used on a bottle of bubbly wine produced in that region of France with a mark identifying the producer (Moet, Veuve Clicquot, Krug, etc.). The important fact is that a (perceived) quality or characteristics of the product be due exclusively or essentially to the geographical environment. In the case of wine this is a combination of the soil, climate and human know-how (together referred to as "*terroir*"). As of November 2015, 28 countries were party to Lisbon, many of them European nations. The protection is granted against usurpation or imitation, even when used in translation or accompanied by words such as "kind", "type" or the like. This means that protection can often apply even where the use would not lead to consumer protection.

As discussed above, the TRIPS Agreement provides for the protection of GIs, a notion similar but not identical to AOs.[267] GIs on wines and

---

267 TRIPS Agreement, Articles 22–24. See D. Gervais, "Reinventing Lisbon: The Case for a Protocol to the Lisbon Agreement", 11(1) *Chicago Journal International Law* (2010), 67–126, at papers. ssrn.com/sol3/papers.cfm?abstract_id=1671676, accessed 26 October 2015.

spirits must be protected at a level approaching Lisbon's, namely even absent consumer deception. Other GIs must be protected when the use is likely to confuse consumers. Under TRIPS, prior trademarks rights can be given priority.[268]

Lisbon members can protect AOs/GIs under a *sui generis* (specific) regime outside of trademark law, as in the European Union, or under certification marks.[269] While the Lisbon system is rather flexible, a number of its provisions have made wide adoption difficult, in particular its rule that an AO cannot be deemed generic in a member if it is generic in its country of origin: a rather rare application of *lex originis* in intellectual property law.[270]

In May 2015, a Diplomatic Conference at WIPO adopted a new version of the Lisbon Agreement, known as the Geneva Act. The Act updates the Lisbon registration system, including by allowing individual member country designation by the applicant (and the payment of per country registration fees – but not the maintenance fees that are typical in the case of trademarks). The Geneva Act maintains the existing rule on genericness. It replaces the protection against usurpation by using language much closer to Article 23 of the TRIPS Agreement, that is protecting all GIs under the Geneva Act without the need to show consumer confusion (a protection level resembling dilution).[271]

It is unclear how the Geneva Act can be implemented by common law jurisdictions that protect geographic symbols of origin under trademark law, often as certification marks. The Lisbon system focuses on producer interests and the maintenance of tradition and the importance of origin in the making of food products (including wines, spirits, beer and mineral water). By contrast, common law trademark systems typically focus and are justified as reflecting consumer interests. This is reflected in the requirement that a mark be used, and in reducing the search costs of consumers in identifying products and services.

268 WTO Panel Report, *European Communities – Protection of Trademarks and Geographical Indications for Agricultural Products and Foodstuffs*, WT/DS290/R, (15 March 2005), at [7.15].

269 See D. Gervais, "A Cognac after Spanish Champagne? Geographical Indications as Certification Marks", in J. C. Ginsburg and R. Dreyfuss (eds.), *Intellectual Property at the Edge* Cambridge: Cambridge University Press 2014, 130–155.

270 Lisbon Agreement for the Protection of Appellations of Origin and their International Registration (1958), Article 6.

271 See D. Gervais, "Irreconcilable Differences? The Geneva Act of the Lisbon Agreement and the Common Law", 53(2) *Houston Law Review* (2016).

5 Key issues in international intellectual property

5.1 International human rights and intellectual property

A number of international agreements on human rights either refer to intellectual property or have become a forum in which the relationship between intellectual property and human rights is discussed. The globalization of intellectual property and the seeming imbalance of rights between developing and developed countries has shone new light on the relationship between intellectual property rights and human rights.[272] The Internet has also contributed to this debate, whereby claims to copyright protection have been seen to conflict with freedom of access to information and freedom of expression. The meaning of human rights and intellectual property issues emerged through discussions within a subcommittee of the United Nations, which set an agenda suggesting there was an extreme conflict between human rights and the TRIPS Agreement.[273]

Intellectual property has been "a normative backwater in the human rights pantheon, neglected by treaty bodies, experts, and commentators while other rights emerged from the jurisprudential shadows".[274] This is certainly true if one looks at human rights treaties that pre-date the TRIPS Agreement by a number of decades. The UDHR provides:

> Everyone has the right freely to participate in the cultural life of the community, to enjoy the arts and to share in scientific advancement and its benefits.

---

272 See C. Geiger (ed.), *A Handbook of Intellectual Property and Human Rights*, Cheltenham: Edward Elgar, 2015.

273 L. R. Helfer, "Human Rights and Intellectual Property: Conflict or Coexistence?", 5 *Minnesota Intellectual Property Review*, (2003), at 47; see also P. Yu, "Reconceptualizing Intellectual Property Interests in a Human Rights Framework", 40 *UC Davis Law Review* (2007), 1039–1049; and generally see G. W. Austin and L. R. Helfer, *Human Rights and Intellectual Property*, Cambridge: Cambridge University Press, 2011.

274 L. R. Helfer, "Human Rights and Intellectual Property: Conflict or Coexistence?", above note 273, at 47.

Everyone has the right to the protection of the moral and material interests resulting from any scientific, literary or artistic production of which he is the author.[275]

Exactly what this means for intellectual property law is not clear. However, the second sentence declares individual rights and the first a kind of group or collective right.[276]

The ICESCR provides to a person a right "to benefit from the protection of the moral and material interests resulting from any scientific, literary or artistic production of which he is the author" and "to enjoy the benefits of scientific progress and its applications".[277]

A significant area of concern has been that the strength of patents over pharmaceuticals is interfering with access to medicines. This has implications related to the right to health. This concern was reflected in amendments to the TRIPS Agreement allowing parallel importation of medicines made under a compulsory license.[278] Concerns over access to medicines and the role of patents in limiting that access remain. This has caused many to look to human rights instruments as a way to create a balance between the interests of owners and users of intellectual property, and has resulted in discussion of human rights and intellectual property concerns in a variety of international fora.[279]

Another way in which the relationship between human rights and intellectual property has emerged is the recognition of intellectual property in the European Union as part of the right to property under the European Convention for the Protection of Human Rights and Fundamental Freedoms.[280] The European Court of Human Rights has recognized human rights in relation to trademarks, patents and copyright.[281]

---

275 Universal Declaration of Human Rights, GA Res A/810 (1948), Article 27.

276 J. Morsink, *The Universal Declaration of Human Rights: Origins, Drafting, and Intent*, Pennsylvania: University of Pennsylvania Press, 1999, at 335.

277 The ICESCR was adopted on 16 December 1966 and entered into force on 3 January 1976. See Article 15(1)(b) and (c); S Exec Doc D, 95-2 at 18; (1977) 993 U.N.T.S. at 3, 9.

278 See discussion of the Doha Declaration and Article 31*bis* in Section [2.2.2].

279 L. R. Helfer, "Regime Shifting: The TRIPS Agreement and New Dynamics of International Intellectual Property Lawmaking", 4(1) *Yale Journal of International Law* (2004), 1.

280 L. R. Helfer, "The New Innovation Frontier? Intellectual Property and the European Court of Human Rights", 49(1) *Harvard International Law Journal* (2008), 1–53.

281 *Ibid.*; and *Anheuser Busch v Portugal* (2007) 45 HRR 830.

5.2   Enforcement of intellectual property rights

5.2.1   Enforcement under the TRIPS Agreement

The enforcement section of the TRIPS Agreement is one of the major achievements of the negotiation. Before TRIPS, provisions dealing with enforcement of rights were basically general obligations to provide for legal remedies and, in certain cases, seizure of infringing goods. In other words, prior to TRIPS, the question was essentially left to national legislation. This was no easy task as civil and criminal procedures tend to vary greatly among WTO members.

TRIPS enforcement provisions can be grouped into five partially overlapping categories:

(1)   General principles of fairness, right to present evidence, right to review, deterrence, balance and reasonable use of available resources within the WTO member concerned, and parity of judicial and administrative procedures.[282]

(2)   Availability of general civil remedies (injunction, damages, destruction of infringing goods or disposal outside the channels of commerce, indemnification of defendant and, where available under national law, the payment by the losing party of the other party's attorneys' fees).[283]

(3)   Availability of provisional remedies (for example, provisional injunctions) *inaudita altera parte* (*ex parte*) in appropriate cases, to seize material, implements and other material.[284]

(4)   A specific – and very detailed for an international text – system to block importation of counterfeit goods at the point of importation (by customs authorities).[285]

(5)   A provision of criminal remedies at least for "wilful trademark counterfeiting or copyright piracy on a commercial scale".[286]

The TRIPS Agreement provides a fair degree of flexibility. It imposes mostly systemic requirements in the sense that WTO members must, in their laws, provide courts and other enforcement authorities with

---

282   TRIPS Agreement, Articles 41–43 and 49. The preambular statement that intellectual property rights are "private rights" is relevant in this context.

283   TRIPS Agreement, Articles 44–48.

284   TRIPS Agreement, Article 50.

285   TRIPS Agreement, Articles 51–60.

286   TRIPS Agreement, Article 61.

certain powers. The Agreement rightly does not require that such powers be exercised in a specific case, as to do so would step too far on the discretion of the authorities (the equitable nature of injunctions in common law jurisdictions comes to mind). The typical phrase used in the TRIPS Agreement is "authorities shall have the authority to. . .".

In the realm of criminal remedies, the notion of commercial scale cabins the scope of the obligation. It is undefined in the TRIPS Agreement, but has been the target of more recent trade negotiations.

The enforcement section was tested when the United States challenged China's enforcement regime in relation to trademarks and copyright.[287] The details of the dispute are complex but, in short, the United States was not successful because the provisions of the TRIPS Agreement did not expressly state the kind of specificity that the United States argued should be found in an enforcement regime. For a number of years the United States and China had been in discussions over enforcement of intellectual property rights in China. These discussions did not result in an agreement about enforcement standards, and so the United States requested the establishment of a WTO panel.

Aspects of the complaint related to the thresholds of infringing copies that would give rise to a criminal level of infringement (infringement on a commercial scale) of copyright and trademarks in China. China reduced the level of the relevant thresholds from 1,000 to 500 shortly before the United States requested a WTO panel. The essence of the United States' case was that China's thresholds for criminal infringement in copyright law were ineffective to meet the TRIPS Agreement requirements that members provide for criminal offences for infringement. Because of the wording of the TRIPS Agreement provisions the United States was not successful in its complaint.

5.2.2 Anti-Counterfeiting Trade Agreement (ACTA)

In 2011 a group of WTO members, including Australia, the United States, the European Union, New Zealand, Canada, Switzerland and Japan, completed negotiation of an agreement about the enforcement of intellectual property rights. Australia, Canada, Japan, Morocco, New Zealand, Singapore, South Korea and the United States

---

287 WTO Panel Report, *China – Measures Affecting the Protection and Enforcement of Intellectual Property Rights*, WT/DS362/R, (26 January 2009).

signed it in October 2011 and in 2012, Mexico, the European Union and 22 of its member states did so as well, but as of June 2015 only one country had formally ratified it, namely Japan. As a result, the Anti-Counterfeiting Trade Agreement (ACTA) has never come into force. Many legislatures and the European Parliament rejected implementing it. Much public outcry about the lack of transparency in the ACTA negotiations resulted in the European Union declining to ratify ACTA, which all but ended any hope of the Agreement's future.[288]

The aim of ACTA was to harmonize rules for enforcement (or at least have more detailed minimum standards) of intellectual property rights found in the TRIPS Agreement. The scope of, for example, criminal liability and remedies for copyright infringement was an area over which there was little international agreement when the TRIPS Agreement was negotiated and subsequently. As a consequence, the enforcement-related minimum standards are not detailed, but broadly provide that there must be some enforcement and remedies.[289]

It is hardly surprising that the United States, in particular, and the European Union should seek greater enforcement standards. The United States has tried to increase enforcement standards in TRIPS negotiations unsuccessfully but with some success through bilateral and FTA negotiations. And, as discussed above, the WTO would not read greater detail into the enforcement provisions. ACTA would likely have existed independent of that dispute, but the failure of the United States to achieve strict enforcement measures through the WTO dispute settlement process arguably fuelled the perceived need for an agreement like ACTA.[290]

---

288 M. Geist, "European parliament reject ACTA: the impossible becomes possible", Michael Geist's Blog, 4 July 2012, at www.michaelgeist.ca/content/view/6578/99999/, accessed 22 April 2015.

289 TRIPS Agreement, Articles 41–60. Article 41(1), the introductory provision to the enforcement articles of the TRIPS Agreement, requires that: "Members shall ensure that enforcement procedures as specified in this Part are available under the law so as to permit effective action against any act of infringement of intellectual property rights covered by this Agreement, including expeditious remedies to prevent infringements and remedies which constitute a deterrent to further infringements. These procedures shall be applied in such a manner as to avoid the creation of barriers to legitimate trade and to provide for safeguards against their abuse."

290 Since the demise of ACTA, another push for a similar treaty has begun by "like-minded" countries in favour of intellectual property maximalism. It is unclear what the results will be, but it is clear that the notion of a TRIPS-Plus agreement has not faded. See, for example, M. Geist, "NDP Calls It: Bill C-56 is 'ACTA Though the Backdoor'", Michael Geist's Blog, 6 March 2012, atwww.michaelgeist.ca/content/view/6800/408/, accessed 22 April 2015.

5.3   Importation rights

5.3.1   Scope of this section

Few areas in intellectual property law are as controversial, both nationally and internationally, as control over what intellectual property can be imported. Preventing the importation of illegally produced intellectual property products is consistent with intellectual property protection in general, and is an appropriate use of the importation right. An important feature of the TRIPS Agreement is its strong emphasis on the signatories providing stronger border control measures to prevent the importation of pirated goods. The controversy, however, has focused on whether intellectual property rights owners ought to be able to prevent legitimate goods produced with their consent in one country from being imported into another country. No agreement was reached on this point.[291] Article 6 of the TRIPS Agreement provides that nothing in the Agreement "shall be used to address the issue of the exhaustion of intellectual property rights".

Such "parallel importation" or "grey marketing" of goods remains a flashpoint in international intellectual property law.[292] For instance, the Supreme Court of the United States decided *Kirtsaeng v John Wiley & Sons, Inc.*[293] In that case, the Court held that US copyright law follows the principle of international exhaustion, meaning that once a book is sold in one country, it may be resold without a license in any other – even when the resale takes place in the United States.

5.3.2   Distinguishing between parallel importation and importation of pirated goods

Intellectual property owners stress the importance of manufacturers' ability to control, through parallel importation restrictions, the distribution of their goods locally or abroad. These distribution rights can be, and often are, presented as a fundamental right of intellectual property owners. For the owners of trademarks, whose very value is often dependent on the quality of the goods themselves or the service pro-

---

291 See V. Chiappetta,"The Desirability of Agreeing to Disagree: The WTO, TRIPS, International IPR Exhaustion and a Few Other Things", 21 *Michigan Journal of International Law* (2000), 333.

292 See generally T. R. Swanson, "Combating Grey Market Goods in a Global Market: Comparative Analysis of Intellectual Property Laws and Recommended Strategies", 22 *Houston Journal of International Law* (2000), 327.

293 *See Kirtsaeng v John Wiley & Sons, Inc.*, 133 S. Ct. 1351, 185 L. Ed. 2d 392 (2013).

vided with the goods, the importation right arguably helps ensure that their goods also receive appropriate promotion and after-sales service.

Copyright and related right owners, especially of sound recordings and computer programs, have similarly argued that parallel importation restrictions greatly assist in preventing the importation of pirated goods. Parallel importation restrictions mean that border enforcement agencies simply need to check whether the importer of particular goods has a license from the copyright owner, rather than making a much more complex inquiry as to whether the goods were legally produced in the country of origin.

Intellectual property owners, however, use parallel importation restrictions to achieve other commercial goals that lie outside the immediate rationales for intellectual property law. These goals include charging different prices in different parts of the world, sometimes but not always based on what locals are able or willing to pay. International price discrimination is primarily a competition law issue, and there are no international agreements regulating it. There is no agreement on whether it is a pro- or anti-competitive practice. It is questionable, however, whether intellectual property law and its territoriality principles are the right mechanisms through which to ensure international price discrimination. Such a use of intellectual property law may result in intellectual property law determining price, rather than the market.

The ability for intellectual property owners to keep these sorts of markets separate depends on parallel import restrictions. Such restrictions can sometimes be anti-competitive and not necessarily consumer friendly. That is especially so in a globalized marketplace, where one of the main principles behind the WTO rules is the free movement of goods and services.

5.3.3   Article 31*bis* of the TRIPS Agreement

In 2001 at the launch of the Doha Round at the WTO, a Declaration on the TRIPS Agreement and Public Health was adopted.[294] Its paragraph 6 instructed the WTO TRIPS Council "to find an expeditious solution"

---

294 WTO, "Declaration on the TRIPS Agreement and public health", WT/MIN(01)/DEC/2, (14 November 2001), at www.wto.org/english/thewto_e/minist_e/min01_e/mindecl_trips_e. htm, accessed 22 April 2015.

to the problem of access to life-saving pharmaceuticals in countries without the ability to manufacture "generic" copies of drugs to
lower costs. Article 31(f) of the TRIPS Agreement prohibits compulsory licenses issued for export purposes. Countries which did have
manufacturing capability could not export to countries (typically least
developed nations) that did not. In 2003 ministers agreed to a solution that allowed the issuance of compulsory licenses for export to
least developed countries.[295] By reference to the 2001 Declaration, it is
often referred to as the "paragraph 6 system". The system also provides
important safeguards to prevent diversion, that is, the re-export of
drugs made for a low-income country to higher income markets.

The paragraph 6 system was added directly into the TRIPS Agreement
in Article 31*bis*. Though that article – the only amendment to TRIPS
since its adoption – was not yet in force as of November 2015,[296] the
system is in place under the 2003 Ministerial Decision.

5.4   International law at the national level: conflict of laws

As if the international intellectual property law system were not
complex enough, each country's national law affects the way it deals
with international law situations. This matter is vastly intricate, but
understanding the basic concept of conflict of laws can serve as an
introduction to this intensely intricate area of law.

5.4.1   Basic conflict of laws concepts

There are several cases where courts in more than one jurisdiction may
be relevant to a dispute. For example, there may be multiple parties in
different states, or the effects of an alleged infringement of an intellectual property right may be felt in more than one territory. In such cases
conflicts may occur. This is referred to as private international law or
simply "conflict of laws". There are few international rules that govern
such conflicts.

---

295 WTO, "Implementation of paragraph 6 of the Doha Declaration on the TRIPS Agreement and
     public health – Decision of the General Council of 30 August 2003", WT/L/540 and Corr.1,
     (1 September 2003), at www.wto.org/english/tratop_e/trips_e/implem_para6_e.htm, accessed
     22 April 2015.
296 54 WTO Members, including the European Union and the United States, had adopted the amend-
     ment. It will enter into force once two-thirds of the WTO's members have accepted the change.

One must distinguish, first, between the issue of jurisdiction and the issue of applicable law. A court may have jurisdiction over a defendant located in its territory but if the infringement occurred in a different territory it may be required, or simply find it more convenient, to apply foreign law. Similarly, contracts often provide for both a choice of venue and a choice of applicable law. Courts in many countries generally respect such choices unless they have a good reason not to do so.

While courts may be persuaded to apply foreign *substantive* law, they often hesitate to do so. One counter-example is contract formation, where the law of the jurisdiction of formation of contract is often applied. The same is true of "status" (for example, marriage, establishment of corporations). Courts will almost always apply their own civil *procedure* rules and remedial measures. For example, a court in a common law jurisdiction will typically consider an injunction an equitable remedy even if a contract provides that a party has a "right" to the remedy. In addition, courts uniformly refuse to apply rules that conflict with *ordre public* and basic principles of their own jurisdictions.

A number of Latin terms are used to refer to the possible laws applicable to a dispute:

- *Lex fori*, the law of the forum where the dispute is litigated
- *Lex loci delicti*, the law of the place of infringement
- *Lex loci protectionis*, the law of the forum where protection is sought
- *Lex originis*, the law of the country or origin (of the work, mark etc.).

Among the few recognized principles applicable to intellectual property disputes, two should be mentioned here:

1. Patents and trademark (registration) are governed by the law of the jurisdiction of the Office that granted the patent or registered the mark. Decisions in other jurisdictions are not binding (principle of independence discussed in Section [4.4.3] above). This also means that only courts in that jurisdiction can invalidate a registered mark or patent. This reflects the fact that in spite of international rules, policy decisions made country by country still matter in this area. As the United States Supreme Court explained in *Microsoft Corp. v AT&T Corp*:

The presumption that United States law governs domestically but does not rule the world applies with particular force in patent law. The traditional understanding that our patent law "operate[s] only domestically and d[oes] not extend to foreign activities", Fisch & Allen ["The Application of Domestic Patent Law to Exported Software: 35 U. S. C. §271(f)", 25 U. Pa. J. Int'l Econ. L. 557 (2004)] 559, is embedded in the Patent Act itself, which provides that a patent confers exclusive rights in an invention within the United States. 35 U. S. C. § 154(a)(1) (patentee's rights over invention apply to manufacture, use, or sale "throughout the United States" and to importation "into the United States"). [. . .] Thus, the United States accurately conveyed in this case [in an amicus curiae brief filed by the US government]: "Foreign conduct is [generally] the domain of foreign law", and in the area here involved, in particular, foreign law "may embody different policy judgments about the relative rights of inventors, competitors, and the public in patented inventions".[297]

2.   In copyright cases, the Berne Convention mandates the application of the *lex loci protectionis*, which is often but not always the *lex fori*. In other words, while this is usually the law of the jurisdiction *in which* protection is claimed, it is in fact the law of the jurisdiction *for which* protection is claimed. For example, Article 5(2) provides in part that "the extent of protection, as well as the means of redress afforded to the author to protect his rights, shall be governed exclusively by the laws of the country where protection is claimed". The law of the "country where protection is claimed" is mentioned on several other occasions in the Convention.[298] It is also mentioned in the 1961 Rome Convention (Article 7(2)) and in the recent Beijing Treaty on Audio-visual Performances (Article 5(3)).

In cases involving a *transmission* (such as via satellite), countries typically opt either for the law of the country of emission (uplink) or the country of reception (downlink). WIPO officials have suggested that the law of emission would apply unless that law is inadequate, in which case the law of the country(ies) of reception would be used.[299]

Though a court may have jurisdiction in a case, it may decline to exercise such jurisdiction under rules based on *comity* or doctrines

---

297 *Microsoft Corp. v AT&T Corp.*, 127 S. Ct. 1746 (2007), 1758.
298 Berne Convention, Articles 6bis(2) and (3), 7(8), 10bis(1), 14bis(2)(a) and (b), 14ter(2) and 18(2).
299 See M. Ficsor, *The Law of Copyright and the Internet*, (Oxford University Press, 2010), at 172–179.

mandating a more convenient forum (*forum non conveniens*). In such cases, a court will voluntarily "cede" jurisdiction to another. This avoids multiple, possibly conflicting, resolutions to the same dispute. Courts are also aware that over-reaching territorially in one case may lead foreign courts to do the same, thus providing a fully self-interested (game-theoretic) reason not to do so. Conversely, a court may be persuaded to look at extra-territorial aspects that are inextricably part of a case, such as a copyright infringement that takes place mostly in one nation but has relatively minor impacts across the border (for example, satellite footprints). In such cases, it may decide to apply the substantive law (for example, defences) of the other country to the foreign situation. This fact pattern is very common on the Internet. There is no uniform standard here. In a 2004 decision, the Supreme Court of Canada suggested a test that seems convincing, however:

> A real and substantial connection to Canada is sufficient to support the application of our Copyright Act to international Internet transmissions in a way that will accord with international comity and be consistent with the objectives of order and fairness.[300]

Finally, one should mention that though there is no comprehensive formal set of rules, efforts have been made to harmonize state practice in this area, including by The Hague Conference on Private International Law which has been negotiating a convention on jurisdiction and foreign judgments in civil and commercial matters that might address intellectual property disputes in various ways;[301] the American Law Institute;[302] and more recently the International Law Association, which established a group called Intellectual Property and Private International Law in November 2010. The principle of "substantial connection" is referred to in many of the documents produced by those groups.[303]

---

300 *Society of Composers, Authors and Music Publishers of Canada v Canadian Assn. of Internet Providers*, [2004] SCC 45, at [60].

301 See R. Dreyfuss and J. C. Ginsburg, "Draft Convention on Jurisdiction and Recognition of Judgments in Intellectual Property Matters", 77 *Chicago-Kent Law Review* (2002), 1065.

302 American Law Institute, *Intellectual Property Principles Governing Jurisdiction, Choice of Law and Judgments in Transnational Disputes*, ALI Publishers 2008.

303 See for example, P. Nygh and F. Pocar, *Preliminary Draft Convention on Jurisdiction and Foreign Judgments in Civil and Commercial Matters*, 2001 Hague Draft, Article 18(1), at www.hcch.net/upload/wop/jdgmpd11.pdf, accessed 15 April 2015. Other notable efforts include the European Max-Planck Group on Conflict of Laws in Intellectual Property (CLIP), the "Transparency Project" and the Japan–Korea Principles Project.

5.5   Traditional knowledge and indigenous resources

The TRIPS Agreement and its incorporated agreements, the Berne Convention and the Paris Convention, do not directly protect traditional knowledge. Some traditional knowledge may fall under one or another intellectual property category. A song, for example, may be a copyright work. Copyright protection is not, however, what those who seek the protection of traditional knowledge claim. The aims of those who seek such protection is that their culture is not offensively treated or misused and that they, rather than others, are able (where the relevant cultural norms permit) to exploit economically and to develop their culture. The protection of traditional knowledge has become a substantial issue in international intellectual property because of the way in which existing and core internationally protected intellectual property rights enable others to make use of, and may even encourage the use of, traditional knowledge. This occurs because the intellectual property system treats traditional knowledge largely as unprotected or, if it ever was, no longer protected by intellectual property law. As global trade in intellectual property and its related products has increased so too has the use (and misuse) of traditional knowledge.

At WIPO there is an ongoing international negotiation on the protection of traditional knowledge. Before discussing that process it is useful to consider what is meant by traditional knowledge and what those who wish for protection are seeking.

5.5.1   The scope of traditional knowledge

A basic working definition of traditional knowledge is:

> intellectual activity in a traditional context, and includes the know-how, skills, innovations, practices and learning that form part of traditional knowledge systems, and knowledge embodying traditional lifestyles of indigenous and local communities, or contained in codified knowledge systems passed between generations and continuously developed following any changes in the environment, geographical conditions and other factors. It is not limited to any specific technical field, and may include agricultural, environmental and medicinal knowledge, and any traditional knowledge associated with cultural expressions and genetic resources.[304]

---

304 WIPO, "The Protection of Traditional Knowledge: Revised Objectives and Principles", WIPO/GRTKF/IC/18/5 (10 January 2011), Annex 18, at www.wipo.int/edocs/mdocs/tk/en/wipo_grtkf_ic_18/wipo_grtkf_ic_18_5.pdf, accessed 23 April 2015.

We describe this as a "working definition" because its primary utility is as a guiding concept rather than as a definition with strict borders. Additionally, the very phrase "traditional knowledge" is in many ways a misnomer. It suggests that the knowledge is only traditional in the sense of old. Much traditional knowledge may be old, but that is only part of the picture. As the working definition shows knowledge is passed from generation to generation (often in traditional ways through stories, skills and as part of daily life). One of the key functions of passing on knowledge is to develop that knowledge for current needs as well as guarding the knowledge for future generations. The use of "traditional" does not mean that the knowledge is an artefact without a modern day function. The goal of protecting some traditional knowledge, such as religious or sacred knowledge, may be for preservation rather than for developmental purposes. That said, what is now internationally called traditional knowledge embodies knowledge which has developed through the ages and which those who seek to protect it now wish to continue to develop.

It is also useful to consider definitions that are used in international agreements and by institutions whose mandate is not primarily about the protection of intellectual property. For example, in the United Nations Declaration on the Rights of Indigenous Peoples the protection of traditional knowledge is described as follows:

> Indigenous peoples have the right to maintain, control, protect and develop their cultural heritage, traditional knowledge and traditional cultural expressions, as well as the manifestations of their sciences, technologies and cultures, including human and genetic resources, seeds, medicines, knowledge of the properties of fauna and flora, oral traditions, literatures, designs, sports and traditional games and visual and performing arts. They also have the right to maintain, control, protect and develop their intellectual property over such cultural heritage, traditional knowledge, and traditional cultural expressions.[305]

5.5.2   Who seeks the protection of traditional knowledge?

Framing who seeks the protection of traditional knowledge contributes to an understanding of what traditional knowledge is and the scope of protection that is sought at international level. Globally,

---

305   United Nations, *United Nations Declaration on the Rights of Indigenous Peoples*, adopted by General Assembly Resolution 61/295 on 13 September 2007, Article 31.

communities that are both small and large seek protection of traditional knowledge. Broadly, there are two groups, with overlaps and sub-groups between and within them. The first broad group is developing countries of all sizes. Large developing countries, such as India, Brazil, Peru and China, all seek international protection of traditional knowledge and many of these countries provide protection in their domestic laws. Small developing countries include, for example, Pacific Island nations such as the Cook Islands, Samoa and Vanuatu and other small states such as Antigua and Barbuda and Puerto Rico. The second broad group seeking international protection is indigenous peoples who reside outside of developing countries and are minority communities in developed countries. These groups are the indigenous peoples of New Zealand, Australia, Canada and the United States. Perhaps unsurprisingly, the interests of these two broad groups (and groups within them) converge on some points and diverge on others. In this overview we refer to those seeking the protection of traditional knowledge as "owners" of that knowledge while recognizing that without legal rights they may not be "owners" as such. Also, often those groups consider themselves to be holders or guardians of the knowledge for the time being. That is, those currently with the use of the knowledge have acquired that status because the knowledge has been passed from previous generations and they have an obligation to preserve and appropriately develop the knowledge and its uses for future generations. The concerns of knowledge guardians are also about inappropriate use of biological and genetic resources, and related traditional knowledge, particularly where the knowledge guardians have an ongoing coexistence and relationship with those resources.

5.5.3 The problem with not protecting traditional knowledge

No protection has meant that others have been free to use traditional knowledge both disrespectfully and also without economic return to those who are the source of the traditional knowledge. Broadly, the reason for this is that the intellectual property system is structured to encourage the use of all that it does not protect. This is what is called the public domain. Traditional knowledge owners often do not share this view of the public domain. Where traditional knowledge has been publicly shared the owners frequently did not consider that such sharing amounted to a relinquishing of custom or control associated with the traditional knowledge.

When intellectual property rights protect traditional knowledge then they either do not provide the protection that the traditional knowledge owners seek, or worse they provide a kind of protection for third parties over adapted aspects of traditional knowledge. It is recognized that intellectual property rules and traditional knowledge do not fit together well, but that does not prevent intellectual property rights from consuming traditional knowledge. That consumption may have a deleterious effect on the knowledge and those whose culture is part of the knowledge, particularly if they can no longer use their knowledge and cannot benefit from its exploitation.

This mismatch of traditional knowledge and intellectual property arises for many reasons. One difficulty is that not all innovative contributions are the same and the existing intellectual property system chooses to recognize innovations in the field of patents that are manifest as useful inventions[306] and in copyright as original works.[307] As far as copyright is concerned, the embodiment of some knowledge assets may not qualify as original works if the art of exact replica is involved. Even where such uses of traditional knowledge do create something which qualifies as a copyright work, copyright does not protect the embodied knowledge from subsequent inappropriate use.[308] As far as patents are concerned, indigenous peoples' innovation often takes the form of "place-based innovation that is cosmologically linked to land and an indigenous group's relationship with that place, rather than to laboratories".[309]

In patent law, traditional knowledge that is relevant to an invention (both products and processes) may be treated as part of the prior art. This means that development of that knowledge within the framework of the customs of the owners of the knowledge may not qualify for patent protection. In patent systems where prior art is usually framed by reference to concepts such as prior publication, traditional knowledge

---

306 TRIPS Agreement, Article 27, requires that patents are available in all fields of technology provided they are new, involve an inventive step (non-obvious) and are capable of industrial application (useful).

307 See Berne Convention, Article 2, incorporated into the TRIPS Agreement, Article 9(1).

308 Understanding this is often best illustrated by use of examples. See the discussion in Chapters 1 and 2, Report of the Waitangi Tribunal (2011), "Ko Aotearoa Tēnei: A Report into Claims Concerning New Zealand Law and Policy Affecting Māori Culture and Identity", at www.waitangi-tribunal.govt.nz/news/media/wai262.asp, accessed 22 April 2015.

309 P. Drahos and S. Frankel, *Indigenous Peoples' Innovation, Intellectual Property Pathways to Development*, Canberra: ANU E-Press, 2012, at 13.

may not be caught in the net and may therefore be treated as not prior art relevant to the assessment of patentability. In this way biological and genetic resources may be used in inventive processes without any recognition of the traditional knowledge that either pointed to that inventive process or is part of the process. There are many examples of this, but perhaps one of the most notorious is that of turmeric, where the well-known uses of it as a wound healing ingredient did not initially stop it from being registered as a patent in both the United States and the European Union (although the patent for the plant-related substance itself was later revoked by the European Patent Office).

In copyright law the concepts which are key to protection, such as the idea/expression dichotomy,[310] suggest that "knowledge" per se is severable from what copyright protects and consequently is free for others to use. In the context of traditional knowledge this would mean that a traditional song or story might on the face of it qualify for copyright protection but that protection does not protect the facts of knowledge conveyed. The protection may also expire and much of the point of traditional knowledge is its ongoing nature both in preserving tradition and developing the knowledge for ongoing uses.

Trademarks protect words and symbols as used in trade, not the knowledge behind those symbols. Thus, traditional knowledge holders may be able to utilize trademarks where they trade, but that does not protect the guardianship or relationship with the knowledge or indeed any situation where the traditional knowledge is not linked to trade.

5.5.4   Possible ways of protecting traditional knowledge and international negotiations

The solution, which is therefore emerging, is not to try and fit traditional knowledge protection into the intellectual property system, but to find protection for it in what is called a *sui generis* system.[311] *Sui generis* rules avoid the problem of having to make general rule changes to intellectual property law, which could have deleterious consequences beyond traditional knowledge (such as giving indefinite protection to all rights) or exceptions within intellectual property law, based on non-intellectual property norms. *Sui generis* regimes may differ from each other. Some may involve pluralistic elements

---

310   TRIPS Agreement, Article 9(2).

311   *Sui generis* means a stand-alone system.

where the customary laws of the traditional knowledge holders are incorporated into the system.[312]

Sui generis systems are not without difficulty because they do not necessarily attract global support and are ineffective in international trade if they are isolated systems. Additionally, *sui generis* protection needs to work effectively with intellectual property law so that one does not defeat the other. In other words, the systems need to effectively interface. In trademark law this might be a mechanism to object to a registration of a trademark that is culturally offensive such as the system in New Zealand.[313] A patent disclosure requirement would also provide an interface between traditional knowledge assets and the patent system. Legal requirements for the disclosure of the origin of biological and genetic resources began in the CBD.[314] In the TRIPS Council, the protection of traditional knowledge was debated as part of a review of Article 27(3)(b) of the TRIPS Agreement. That also included a discussion on the relationship between the TRIPS Agreement and the CBD.[315] There is little agreement between members of the WTO on this relationship. An added complexity is that the discussions have been tied to equally controversial discussions over the protection of GIs, over which the European Union and the United States do not agree.[316] Many developed countries are opposed to any form of compulsory disclosure requirement in patent law. The United States, for example, is of the view that there is no conflict between the CBD (it has not ratified the CBD) and the TRIPS Agreement and has suggested that any issue of access to genetic resources and benefit-sharing can and should be resolved through contracts.[317]

---

312 See Ko Aotearoa Tēnei, above note 308.

313 Trade Marks Act 2002 (NZ), s 17 (1)(c). See also Susy Frankel, "Trademarks and Traditional Knowledge and Cultural Intellectual Property Rights" in Graeme B. Dinwoodie and Mark D. Janis (eds) *Trademark Law and Theory* (Edward Elgar, 2008).

314 See discussion at Section [2.2.2].

315 See generally WTO, "Article 27.3b, traditional knowledge, biodiversity", at www.wto.org/english/tratop_e/trips_e/art27_3b_e.htm, accessed 22 April 2015. See also D. Gervais, *TRIPS Agreement Drafting History and Analysis*, 4th edn., London: Sweet & Maxwell 2012, paras. 1.79–1.94.

316 See Section [3.6.2] on GIs and the three-step test.

317 Council for Trade-Related Aspects of Intellectual Property Rights, "Communication from the United States: Article 27:3 (b), Relationship between the Convention on Biological Diversity and the TRIPS Agreement", IP/C/W/257, (13 June 2001). See also J. Carr, "Agreements that Divide: TRIPS vs. CBD and Proposals for Mandatory Disclosure of Source and Origin of Genetic Resources in Patent Applications", 18 *Journal of Transnational Law and Policy* (2008), 131, at 144–148; "'Ka Mate Ka Mate' and the Protection of Traditional Knowledge"

5.5.5   WIPO and traditional knowledge

The members of WIPO meet as an intergovernmental committee (WIPO-IGC) to discuss the protection of traditional knowledge. The WIPO-IGC has an extensive negotiation process underway for treaties to protect traditional knowledge, both as it relates to biological and genetic resources and to traditional cultural expressions (TCEs).[318]

The WIPO-IGC negotiations include evolving objectives and principles which have become the basis of draft treaties in the areas of both TCEs and genetic resources.[319] With regard to traditional knowledge and TCEs a key objective includes providing beneficiaries with appropriate legal measures and practical means to prevent the misappropriation and misuse/offensive and derogatory use of their TCEs and to give them greater control over uses of their traditional knowledge.[320] At the time of writing these negotiations are ongoing.

5.6   Bilateral and plurilateral trade agreements

The 1993 North American Free Trade Agreement (NAFTA), chapter 17, is a prime example of a trade agreement that deals with intellectual property.[321] Its members are Canada, Mexico and the United States. Chapter 17 of NAFTA is in many ways similar to the TRIPS text. This is not surprising as both TRIPS and NAFTA were based on the same set of industry submissions. Issues that were "pushed" by non-NAFTA members in the TRIPS context, such as GIs – a European Union-led topic – are in the TRIPS Agreement, but not in NAFTA.

---

in Rochelle Dreyfuss and Jane Ginsburg (eds) *Intellectual Property at the Edge*, Cambridge: Cambridge University Press, 2013.

318 For WIPO's work see generally online at: www.wipo.int, accessed 22 April 2015.

319 The latest versions can be found at www.wipo.int/tk/en/igc/, accessed 22 April 2015.

320 WIPO Intergovernmental Committee on Intellectual Property and Genetic Resources, Traditional Knowledge and Folklore, Document prepared by the secretariat, "The Protection of Traditional Cultural Expressions: Draft Articles", WIPO/GRTKF/IC/25/7, (19 July 2013), Annex, page 2, para 1.

321 North American Free Trade Agreement Between the Government of Canada, the Government of Mexico and the Government of the United States, 17 December 1992, Can. T. S. 1994 No. 2, (entered into force 1 January 1994), at www.wipo.int/wipolex/en/other_treaties/details.jsp?treaty_id=232, accessed 22 April 2015 (hereinafter NAFTA).

As discussed above contrary to treaties administered by WIPO, such as the Paris, Berne and Rome Conventions,[322] the TRIPS Agreement is part of the WTO framework. As such, when countries disagree about the implementation or application of the Agreement, they can have recourse to the WTO binding dispute settlement mechanism. NAFTA is an example of a trade agreement that has a state to state dispute settlement system for its intellectual property chapter (chapter 17) and it also contains "investor-state" protection, an issue discussed in the next section.

Since the TRIPS Agreement, a number of regional and bilateral proposals have attempted to impose standards beyond those contained in TRIPS. Hence, they are often referred to as "TRIPS-Plus". They are often negotiated at the behest of the European Union and the United States to protect intellectual property exporters located in their territories. For example, TRIPS-Plus standards are contained in bilateral agreements signed by the United States with Australia, Central America, Korea and Singapore.[323] These instruments include commitments not to use certain flexibilities contained in the TRIPS Agreement, additional rights (for example, in the digital copyright realm), limits on the use of pharmaceutical price controls and investor-state protection. Agreements with the European Union typically add heightened protection for GIs, such as in the Comprehensive Economic and Trade Agreement between Canada and the European Union, which was released in 2014 and was undergoing translation and as of this writing (October 2015). Ratification is delayed pending other trade negotiations, in particular the Trans-Atlantic Trade and Investment Partnership.

Efforts have also emerged at a broader level, such as the ACTA concluded in October 2011 and signed by Australia, Canada, the European Union (and 22 of its member states), Japan, Mexico, Morocco,

---

322 The Rome Convention is jointly administered by WIPO, UNESCO and the ILO.

323 Respectively: Central America–Dominican Republic–United States Free Trade Agreement, 28 May 2004, at www.ustr.gov/trade-agreements/free-trade-agreements/cafta-dr-dominican-republic-central-america-fta/final-text, accessed 22 April 2015; United States–Australia Free Trade Agreement, 18 May 2004, at www.ustr.gov/trade-agreements/free-trade-agreements/australian-fta/final-text, accessed 22 April 2015; Free Trade Agreement Between the United States and Republic of Korea, 30 June 2007, at www.ustr.gov/trade-agreements/free-trade-agreements/korus-fta/final-text, accessed 22 April 2015; and United States–Singapore Free Trade Agreement, 6 May 2003, at www.ustr.gov/sites/default/files/uploads/agreements/fta/singapore/asset_upload_file708_4036.pdf, accessed 22 April 2015.

New Zealand, Singapore, South Korea and the United States after years of controversial secretive negotiations. The Agreement is likely never to enter into force.[324] Renewed efforts to agree TRIPS-Plus norms have been negotiated in the Trans-Pacific Partnership, involving Australia, Brunei, Canada, Chile, Japan, Malaysia, Mexico, New Zealand, Peru, Singapore, the United States and Vietnam. Trans-Pacific Partnership negotiations, including on its intellectual property chapter, were also conducted secretly. The agreed text was revealed in November 2015 but at present, its members have not implemented and ratified the agreement.

These sorts of trade agreements are controversial for many reasons including that they serve to increase standards without multilateral negotiations.

5.7   Intellectual property as a cross-border investment asset

Intellectual property is now included as a "protected investment" or "asset" in investment agreements.[325] These agreements are in two forms; bilateral investment treaties (known as BITs) and investment chapters in FTAs. These agreements provide rights for investors against expropriation for and unfair treatment of their assets. Disputes under these agreements are heard in investment tribunals which allow private litigant ("investors") to bring actions against states in which their investment is based. This is known as investor-state dispute settlement. Investment agreements, therefore, give some intellectual property rights owners additional rights and an international venue other than the WTO dispute settlement process to bring their disputes.

What this means in the context of intellectual property law is not yet fully realized, in part because there have been few cases. An investment tribunal, convened for a dispute under NAFTA, held that participation in the regulatory system around approval for pharmaceutical marketing did not amount to an investment covered by the

---

324 As of March 2015, it had only been ratified by one signatory (Japan).

325 See for example Treaty Concerning the Encouragement and Reciprocal Protection of Investment, US–El Salvador, Article 1, 10 March 1991, S. Treaty Doc. 106-28 (2000) (defining protected investments as including intellectual property).

agreement.[326] At the time of writing there are two investment disputes before arbitral tribunals about trademarks as investment assets, relating to the Australian legislation mandating the plain packaging of cigarettes. These disputes have been brought by the tobacco company Philip Morris respectively against the government of Australia under the Australia–Hong Kong BIT and against the government of Uruguay under a Swiss–Uruguay BIT.[327]

Another investment matter has been brought by a pharmaceutical company, Eli Lilly, against the government of Canada, under the investment chapter of NAFTA.[328] That dispute concerns the Canadian patent system and the basis on which the Patent Office and several courts have revoked two patents because the patents did not, after full examination,[329] meet the criteria for patentability under Canadian law, specifically the law relating to utility.

As part of these disputes investment tribunals are called upon to interpret the relevance of the parties' obligations under the TRIPS Agreement and other trade obligations. This is because often the definition of investment asset utilizes the international agreements relating to intellectual property. This raises the possibility of conflicting interpretations between investment tribunals and the WTO. Fundamentally, the object and purpose of investment agreements is different from the object and purpose of the TRIPS Agreement and its substantive incorporated treaties (the Berne and Paris Conventions). Thus, the interpretations may serve different purposes given the different nature of disputes. However, ideally the interpretation of international obligations should be consistent between international bodies.

---

326 Apotex Inc. vs. United States, Award on Jurisdiction and Admissibility, pp. 209–10, 222–23 (NAFTA/UNCITRAL Arb. Trib., 14 June 2013).

327 For discussion of these case see Valentina S. Vadi, "Global Health Governance at A Crossroads: Trademark Protection v. Tobacco Control in International Investment Law", 48 *Stanford Journal of Int'l Law* (2012), 93.

328 Eli Lilly and Company v. Canada (ICSID Case No. UNCT/14/2).

329 In most jurisdictions patents even if initially registered always remain subject to the possibility of revocation as part of a full examination or litigation involving questions of patent validity.

Final thoughts

International intellectual property law is a dynamic and complex area. From a set of technical and arcane rules reserved for experts, the intersection of intellectual property law with high profile issues such as online uses of material (often protected by copyright) and public health (patents on pharmaceuticals, tobacco regulation) have greatly increased awareness among members of the public. This has prompted a significant amount of empirical and theoretical research on the positive and negative effects of intellectual property law and the need for regulators to strike an appropriate balance. Many recent efforts and models were premised on the need for international intellectual property rules not just to allow companies to capture additional rents in new markets but more broadly to foster economic and human development in a way that reflects in an appropriate way the cultural, historical, educational and other differences among nations and regions. On the economic front, the economies of many countries have moved or are in the process of moving towards the creation of intangibles or at least using intellectual property law to protect innovation in various forms. Intellectual property law impacts human creativity, scientific endeavour, and the business and cultural norms and institutions around such activity. In this book we have given an overview of the key (mainly legal) principles that govern the area. Many of those principles have a long history and are considered steadfast pillars of intellectual property law. The changes and challenges relate to how those principles are applied and updated or adjusted (or indeed lag behind) current global developments.

Index